Choose JESUS

3-MINUTE DEVOTIONS FOR TEEN GIRLS

© 2024 by Barbour Publishing, Inc.

ISBN 979-8-89151-006-7

All rights reserved. No part of this publication may be reproduced or transmitted for commercial purposes, except for brief quotations in printed reviews, without written permission of the publisher. Reproduced text may not be used on the World Wide Web. No Barbour Publishing content may be used as artificial intelligence training data for machine learning, or in any similar software development.

Churches and other noncommercial interests may reproduce portions of this book without the express written permission of Barbour Publishing, provided that the text does not exceed 500 words or 5 percent of the entire book, whichever is less, and that the text is not from material quoted from another publisher. When reproducing text from this book, include the following credit line: "From *Choose Jesus: 3-Minute Devotions for Teen Girls*, published by Barbour Publishing, Inc. Used by permission."

Scripture quotations marked NKJV are taken from the New King James Version®. Copyright © 1982 by Thomas Nelson, Inc. Used by permission. All rights reserved.

Scripture quotations marked NIV are taken from the HOLY BIBLE, NEW INTERNATIONAL VERSION®. NIV®. Copyright © 1973, 1978, 1984, 2011 by Biblica, Inc.™ Used by permission. All rights reserved worldwide.

Scripture quotations marked NLV are taken from the New Life Version copyright © 1969 and 2003 by Barbour Publishing, Inc., Uhrichsville, Ohio, 44683. All rights reserved.

Scripture quotations marked ESV are from The Holy Bible, English Standard Version®, copyright © 2001 by Crossway Bibles, a publishing ministry of Good News Publishers. The ESV® text has been reproduced in cooperation with and by permission of Good News Publishers. Unauthorized reproduction of this publication is prohibited. All rights reserved.

Scripture quotations marked NLT are taken from the *Holy Bible*. New Living Translation copyright© 1996, 2004, 2015 by Tyndale House Foundation. Used by permission of Tyndale House Publishers, Inc. Carol Stream, Illinois 60188. All rights reserved.

Scripture quotations marked CEV are from the Contemporary English Version, Copyright © 1995 by American Bible Society. Used by permission.

Published by Barbour Publishing, Inc., 1810 Barbour Drive, Uhrichsville, Ohio 44683, www.barbourbooks.com

Our mission is to inspire the world with the life-changing message of the Bible.

Printed in China.

Choose JESUS

3-MINUTE DEVOTIONS FOR TEEN GIRLS

JOANNE SIMMONS

BARBOUR
PUBLISHING

Introduction

The very best thing you can ever do is choose Jesus! There is no one else like the Savior! Within these pages, you'll be guided through just-right-size readings that point you to Him and that you can experience in as few as three minutes:

Minute 1: Reflect on God's Word

Minute 2: Read real-life application and encouragement

Minute 3: Pray

These devotions aren't meant to be a replacement for digging deep into the scriptures or for personal, in-depth quiet time. Instead, consider them a perfect jump start to help you form a habit of spending time with Jesus and learning more about Him every day. Or add them to the time you're already spending with Him. Share these moments with friends, family, and others you come in contact with every day. Everyone needs to choose Jesus!

Jesus said, "I am the Way and the Truth and the Life. No one can go to the Father except by Me."
JOHN 14:6 NLV

Why Choose Jesus? Part 1

[Jesus said:] "I am going away to make a place for you. After I go and make a place for you, I will come back and take you with Me. Then you may be where I am. You know where I am going and you know how to get there." Thomas said to Jesus, "Lord, we do not know where You are going. How can we know the way to get there?"
JOHN 14:2–5 NLV

People say this kind of thing all the time when someone dies: "He's in a better place now." Or "She's finally at peace." Or "Heaven gained another angel." We all have the hope that there is peaceful and perfect life after death for our loved ones and for ourselves—but how can we be sure? The answer is Jesus. And that's why we should choose Him.

Jesus, I want to know more about You through Your Word and through prayer. Please guide me and teach me and draw me closer to You. Amen.

Why Choose Jesus? Part 2

Jesus said, "I am the Way and the Truth and the Life. No one can go to the Father except by Me. If you had known Me, you would know My Father also. From now on you know Him and have seen Him."
JOHN 14:6–7 NLV

Jesus Christ alone offers us the promises we can believe in forever. He is "the Way and the Truth and the Life." This crazy world often doesn't make much sense. It's popular to say, "Live your truth." But think about it. . .if everyone and everything can be true, then nothing is true. Right can be wrong, and wrong can be right just based on feelings and opinions. That makes for chaos. There has to be one ultimate source of good truth, and that comes from God Himself, who came to us in human form in the person of Jesus Christ. He is the way through this life to guide us to God. He is the one and only truth. And He alone offers us perfect forever life.

Jesus, I believe in You as the one and only way, truth, and life. I believe that Your written Word, the Bible, is our guide. Please lead me in it. Amen.

The Beginning of Sin

*Everyone has sinned; we all fall
short of God's glorious standard.*
ROMANS 3:23 NLT

When God created everything, including the first two people, Adam and Eve, He didn't make them robots programmed to do His bidding. He gave them free will—the ability to choose to love Him and obey His good guidance or not. He wants love and devotion from people that is chosen and real, not forced and fake. Adam and Eve chose to disobey Him, and ever since, sin has been spreading everywhere. And there's a big price to pay for sin—suffering and death. But God still loved people in spite of sin, and He knew we would need a way to choose to be right with Him again. So He sent Jesus to be our Savior.

---

*Father God, You are Creator, and You are perfect!
Thank You for loving people in spite of all our sin.
Thank You for sending Your Son, Jesus, and giving
me and all people the free will to choose Him! Amen.*

Jesus Makes Us Right with God

We are made right with God by placing our faith in Jesus Christ. And this is true for everyone who believes, no matter who we are. For everyone has sinned; we all fall short of God's glorious standard. Yet God, in his grace, freely makes us right in his sight. He did this through Christ Jesus when he freed us from the penalty for our sins. For God presented Jesus as the sacrifice for sin.
ROMANS 3:22–25 NLT

Like Adam and Eve, we choose bad behavior and disobedience to God sometimes in our own unique ways. We hurt others. We act rude. We say mean things. We lie or cheat in big or small ways. We get jealous. The list goes on and on. But the Father who made us, the one true Creator God, is perfect. We all need relationship with Him. And the only way to be right with Him and have relationship with Him is through Jesus Christ, whom He sent to pay the price for our sin.

Jesus, thank You that You make it possible to be right with God because You died on the cross to pay for my sin. Amen.

Jesus Is Our Only Savior from Sin

For the sin of this one man, Adam, caused death to rule over many. But even greater is God's wonderful grace and his gift of righteousness, for all who receive it will live in triumph over sin and death through this one man, Jesus Christ.
ROMANS 5:17 NLT

Jesus willingly gave up His life on the cross and died to pay for our sin. When we admit our sin and trust in Him as our Savior, we are given the most amazing gift of grace, which covers our sin, plus new life that lasts forever. We begin our new life in Christ as soon as we allow Him to be our Lord and choose to follow and obey Him.

Jesus, I know I'm a sinner, and I'm sorry. I need Your forgiveness and grace. Thank You for dying on the cross to pay the penalty for my sin. Thank You that You rose to life again. Thank You for freedom from sin and for the promise of eternal life. Thank You for making me right with God. I choose You, and I choose to live for You, Jesus. Amen.

Choose Jesus, Choose the Holy Spirit

[Jesus said:] "The Helper is the Holy Spirit. The Father will send Him in My place. He will teach you everything and help you remember everything I have told you."
JOHN 14:26 NLV

After Jesus died, He rose and returned to heaven, but God didn't just leave us alone in the world. He gave us the Holy Spirit. When you choose Jesus as Savior and Lord of your life, you receive the Holy Spirit into your life. The Holy Spirit is your comforter, your counselor, your guide, and so much more. The Holy Spirit cares for you and even prays for you when you don't know what to pray. (See Romans 8:26–28 for more about that!)

Jesus, I'm so glad You are always with me through the presence of the Holy Spirit. I am never alone, never forgotten, never without Your help and hope. Help me to sense Your Holy Spirit every single moment, in every single thing I do, and help me to listen well to Your wisdom and leading. Amen.

The Fruit of the Holy Spirit

The Holy Spirit produces this kind of fruit in our lives: love, joy, peace, patience, kindness, goodness, faithfulness, gentleness, and self-control.
GALATIANS 5:22–23 NLT

When you choose Jesus and thus the Holy Spirit, you can start living the very best kind of life—life filled with good fruit! Not from the bowl on your counter or the produce section at the grocery store but the good fruit that God's Word describes. More love, joy, peace, patience, kindness, goodness, faithfulness, gentleness, and self-control in your mind, heart, and actions are all evidence that the Holy Spirit is living in you and making you increasingly like Jesus every day! What are the ways you can sense and see this fruit filling your life, and how are you sharing it with others?

Jesus, I praise You for the Holy Spirit filling me and producing good fruit in my life. Thank You for making me a better person each and every day as I grow more and more in my relationship with You. I pray others see that difference that You make in my life and want to trust in You as Savior and live for You too! Amen.

Jesus Teaches Us How to Pray, Part 1

[Jesus] said to them, "When you pray, say: 'Father, hallowed be your name. Your kingdom come. Give us each day our daily bread, and forgive us our sins, for we ourselves forgive everyone who is indebted to us. And lead us not into temptation.' "
LUKE 11:2–4 ESV

Praying doesn't come easily sometimes, especially if you're just starting out in your relationship with God through Jesus Christ. It might feel really awkward. But Jesus gave us a clear, straightforward example of how to pray. First, we should spend time praising God and His holy name. We should ask for His kingdom to come, His will to be done. We should ask for our daily needs to be met. We should ask for forgiveness of our sins plus help and reminders to forgive others who sin against us. And we should ask for protection against temptation and sin. Is this the only way to pray? No, but it's Jesus' specific example, and we can let it guide us every moment as we talk to God.

Jesus, please keep bringing me back to Your teaching about prayer to guide me in good communication with You. Amen.

Jesus Teaches Us How to Pray, Part 2

[Jesus said:] "Suppose you went to a friend's house at midnight, wanting to borrow three loaves of bread. You say to him, 'A friend of mine has just arrived for a visit, and I have nothing for him to eat.' And suppose he calls out from his bedroom, 'Don't bother me. . . .' But I tell you this—though he won't do it for friendship's sake, if you keep knocking long enough, he will get up and give you whatever you need because of your shameless persistence. And so I tell you, keep on asking, and you will receive what you ask for. Keep on seeking, and you will find. Keep on knocking, and the door will be opened to you."
LUKE 11:5–9 NLT

Jesus taught us to be persistent in prayer, so keep at it! As long as our requests don't go against His ways and His will, He hears us and wants to bless us with them. And if you're not sure if what you're asking Him goes against His ways and His will, keep reading His Word and asking Him to show you.

Jesus, I will keep on praying to You! Thank You! Amen.

Jesus Teaches Us How to Pray, Part 3

[Jesus said:] "Would any of you fathers give your son a stone if he asked for bread? Or would you give a snake if he asked for a fish? Or if he asked for an egg, would you give him a small animal with a sting of poison? You are sinful and you know how to give good things to your children. How much more will your Father in heaven give the Holy Spirit to those who ask Him?"
LUKE 11:11–13 NLV

Jesus continued to teach about prayer in this way: if human dads who love their kids want to give them good gifts, how much more would our Creator, who is the one and only perfect loving Father, want to give us good gifts when we ask Him? If you believe in Jesus as the Savior who paid the price for your sin, you are in close relationship with your heavenly Father. And His Word promises He wants to bless you with the very best kind of gifts—and those best gifts are found through the Holy Spirit working in your life.

Jesus, thank You for teaching me about prayer and good gifts. Amen.

Scripture Keeps Us Close to Jesus

You have been taught the holy Scriptures from childhood, and they have given you the wisdom to receive the salvation that comes by trusting in Christ Jesus. All Scripture is inspired by God and is useful to teach us what is true and to make us realize what is wrong in our lives. It corrects us when we are wrong and teaches us to do what is right. God uses it to prepare and equip his people to do every good work.
2 Timothy 3:15–17 nlt

We can keep in close relationship with Jesus by constantly learning from His Word. We can trust that every bit of the Bible is inspired by God. With His Word, He corrects us, prepares us, and equips us for every good thing He has planned for us. We should regularly spend time reading the Bible and praying in a manner similar to the prayer below:

Jesus, through scripture today, please teach me more about You and how You want me to live. Please give me wisdom, knowledge, and more understanding. Encourage me and show me Your awesome love, protection, and care. Amen.

The Two Greatest Commandments

"Teacher, what is the most important commandment in the Law?" Jesus answered: Love the Lord your God with all your heart, soul, and mind. This is the first and most important commandment. The second most important commandment is like this one. And it is, "Love others as much as you love yourself."
MATTHEW 22:36–39 CEV

Jesus said the two most important commandments to obey are to love God first with all your heart, soul, and mind and to love your neighbor as yourself. If you focus on obeying these commandments, you will automatically do other things well too. Sometimes you'll hear people say something like "Jesus just says to love everyone. That's all you have to do." But they ignore the fact that Jesus said we are to love God first and most of all. We can't love others in the best ways that God intended unless we first love God with all our heart, soul, and mind—and that includes getting to know Him through His Word and through prayer.

Jesus, above everything else in my life, I want to obey these greatest commandments You taught. Please help me to stay focused. Amen.

Jesus throughout the Bible

He took up our pain and bore our suffering. . . .
He was pierced for our transgressions, he was crushed
for our iniquities; the punishment that brought us
peace was on him, and by his wounds we are healed.
ISAIAH 53:4–5 NIV

Jesus wasn't physically born into the world yet in the Old Testament of the Bible, but He is present throughout the Old Testament in the ways He is prophesied about and in other specific ways too. (See Luke 24:25–27, Acts 26:22–23, and 1 Peter 1:10–12.) Isaiah 53 describes how He would take on our pain and suffering and the punishment for sin and be wounded in order to heal and save us from sin. And all of that was fulfilled through His death on the cross and resurrection.

Jesus, when I'm reading any book of the Bible,
please help me see and understand how it all
points toward You as the one and only hope of the
world, the one and only Savior from sin. Amen.

Confession Time

I cried out to him for help, praising him as I spoke. If I had not confessed the sin in my heart, the Lord would not have listened. But God did listen! He paid attention to my prayer.
PSALM 66:17–19 NLT

The Lord is all-knowing and hears our thoughts and prayers—every single one. But if we truly want Him to listen and answer us, we must regularly admit our sins, not hold on to them (or "cherish" them, as some versions of this scripture put it). The Bible promises that God forgives us and removes our sin as far as the east is from the west (Psalm 103:12), but first we must confess those sins. That keeps us humble and depending on Jesus and His saving grace, which is the very best blessing—to be dependent on the one who loved (and continues to love) us so much that He was willing to die for us.

Jesus, You know I make many mistakes, and I don't want to hide them or pretend like I don't sin. These are my sins I've been struggling with: _____. Please forgive me for them and remove them from me. Thank You! Amen.

Choose Baptism

Jesus came to them and said: I have been given all authority in heaven and on earth! Go to the people of all nations and make them my disciples. Baptize them in the name of the Father, the Son, and the Holy Spirit, and teach them to do everything I have told you.
MATTHEW 28:18–20 CEV

Once you choose Jesus as your Savior, it's important to choose to be baptized. It's not something you absolutely *have* to do to be saved and go to heaven forever. For example, the man next to Jesus on the cross never had a chance to be baptized, yet Jesus promised the man he would be with Him that day in paradise (Luke 23:42–43). But if you do have a chance, it is right to obey God's Word and follow Jesus' example. Baptism is a symbol of choosing new life with Jesus. It's a way to show that you want to obey God and be like Jesus, that you are saved from sin and are His follower!

Jesus, I want to obey You about baptism and show others how much I love You and want to live my life for You! Amen.

Take Jesus at His Word

Jesus told him, "Go back home. Your son will live!"
JOHN 4:50 NLT

The government official in the story in John 4 had legal authority over Jesus, but he respected Jesus. He came to Jesus and begged Him to heal his son who was sick. And Jesus said, "Go back home. Your son will live!" With his authority, the official could have ordered Jesus to come to his son in person to heal him. But the official decided to believe Jesus had the miraculous power to heal from anywhere, even from afar, and he trusted Jesus would do it. He took Jesus at His word and headed home.

While the official was still traveling, some of his servants met him along the way and told him his son was well again. The official asked, "What time did he get better?" When his servants named the time, the official realized that was the exact time that Jesus had said to him, "Your son will live." From then on, not only did the official believe in Jesus but so did everyone in his household.

Jesus, I choose to take You at Your word. Amen.

Our One and Only Savior

Jesus is holy and has no guilt. He has never sinned and is different from sinful men. He has the place of honor above the heavens. Christ is not like other religious leaders. They had to give gifts every day on the altar in worship for their own sins first and then for the sins of the people. Christ did not have to do that. He gave one gift on the altar and that gift was Himself. It was done once and it was for all time.
HEBREWS 7:26–27 NLV

Have you ever heard people say that all religions are the same? If you spend even a small amount of time learning about other religions, you realize it's just not true. Belief in Jesus as God and as our one and only Savior is the one true religion. Jesus alone was (and is) perfect and holy and without sin. He gave His own life once for all for people of all time, and no other religion offers that kind of gift and love and miracle!

Jesus, there is truly no one else like You! You are God, and You are the one true Savior! Thank You for giving Your life to save everyone who believes in You! Amen.

Go to Church

We must hold tightly to the hope we say is ours. After all, we can trust the one who made the agreement with us. We should keep on encouraging each other to be thoughtful and to do helpful things. Some people have given up the habit of meeting for worship, but we must not do that. We should keep on encouraging each other, especially since you know that the day of the Lord's coming is getting closer.
HEBREWS 10:23–25 CEV

The Bible tells us that we need to meet together regularly with other Christians who choose to trust Jesus as their Savior too. We need to worship and learn more about God together; and we need to encourage, comfort, and take good care of each other!

Jesus, thank You for all the other Christians who are in my life and for those all over the world! Help us to love getting together at church to grow closer to You and to each other. Amen.

Triune God

In the beginning was the Word, and the Word was with God, and the Word was God. He was in the beginning with God. All things were made through him, and without him was not any thing made that was made.... And the Word became flesh and dwelt among us, and we have seen his glory, glory as of the only Son from the Father, full of grace and truth.
JOHN 1:1–3, 14 ESV

Jesus has always existed and has always been God because God is triune, meaning existing in three—Father, Son, and Holy Spirit—who are distinct but equal. So we learn about Jesus throughout the whole Bible.

Jesus, as I read Your Word, show me all the great things I can learn about You throughout both Old Testament and New. I want to know You better and follow You every day. Amen.

You Are the Light

"You are the light of the world—like a city on a hilltop that cannot be hidden. No one lights a lamp and then puts it under a basket. Instead, a lamp is placed on a stand, where it gives light to everyone in the house. In the same way, let your good deeds shine out for all to see, so that everyone will praise your heavenly Father."
MATTHEW 5:14–16 NLT

The light of the world—that's a big deal! That's what Jesus has said about you and all believers when we trust Him as Savior. With the Holy Spirit living inside us, our job is to shine our lights that point to Him so that others will want to trust Jesus as Savior and praise God too! We should never want to conceal our light. So many people in the dark world around us need the good news and love of Jesus, so we need to shine as brightly as possible!

Jesus, it's incredible to be the light of the world because of You! I want to shine Your love brightly to everyone around me and give God all the praise! Amen.

Jesus Often Taught in Parables

His disciples came and asked him, "Why do you use parables when you talk to the people?"
MATTHEW 13:10 NLT

Jesus answered this question: "This is why I speak to them in picture-stories. They have eyes but they do not see. They have ears but they do not hear and they do not understand. It happened in their lives as Isaiah said it would happen. He said, 'You hear and hear but do not understand. You look and look but do not see. . . . They hear very little with their ears. They have closed their eyes. If they did not do this, they would see with their eyes and hear with their ears and understand with their hearts. Then they would be changed in their ways, and I would heal them'" (Matthew 13:13–15 NLV).

Remember this answer from Jesus, and pray for understanding as you study His parables, His example, and all the writings in the Bible. We want to have eyes, ears, minds, and hearts that are open and paying attention so we understand how God is trying to teach us.

Jesus, please give me understanding as I read Your Word and learn from Your teaching. Amen.

Choose to Be a Child of God

See what great love the Father has lavished on us, that we should be called children of God! And that is what we are!
1 JOHN 3:1 NIV

When we choose to trust in Jesus as Savior, we can have a close relationship with God as our heavenly Father. It's so wonderful to have earthly family, but it's even better to know we are in the family of the one true Almighty God. Sometimes troubles in earthly families get totally out of control. Earthly families can break apart. So being part of God's family is especially important because we know that no matter what goes on in earthly families, we are always God's children—and *no one* can break that bond. With the one true Almighty God as our loving Father, we have all His care and protection every single day of our lives.

Jesus, I'm so thankful that because of You, I'm a child of Almighty God, who loves and takes good care of me now and forever. Amen.

Jesus Is "God with Us"

"She will give birth to a son, and they will call him Immanuel, which means 'God is with us.'"
MATTHEW 1:23 NLT

The name for Jesus, Immanuel, means "God is with us," which is so encouraging. Remembering and celebrating the fact that Jesus came to be here on earth with us and knows our struggles and fears as human beings firsthand is comforting. God is with us every moment. No, we weren't alive during Jesus' time as a human on earth, but we trust that He was here and experienced a human life like we are now. And today we have His Word and the Holy Spirit to help us live for Him until our time on earth is finished or He returns again, whichever comes first.

Jesus Immanuel, You understand me because You came to be a human and lived in this world too. Please help me trust, depend on, and relate to You more each day. Amen.

Jesus' Mother, Mary

The angel said to her, "Mary, do not be afraid. You have found favor with God. See! You are to become a mother and have a Son. You are to give Him the name Jesus."
LUKE 1:30–31 NLV

When Mary was told she would be the mother of Jesus, she was scared and confused at first. But once her questions were answered, she said, "I am willing to be used of the Lord. Let it happen to me as you have said" (Luke 1:38 NLV). And when she shared the news with her cousin Elizabeth, she said: "Oh, how my soul praises the Lord. How my spirit rejoices in God my Savior! For he took notice of his lowly servant girl, and from now on all generations will call me blessed. For the Mighty One is holy, and he has done great things for me. He shows mercy from generation to generation to all who fear him" (Luke 1:46–50 NLT).

Jesus, when You ask me to do big things, help me to worship You, thank You, and trust You to equip me to do exactly what You call me to. Amen.

Let Jesus Lead You

The Lord is my shepherd, I lack nothing. He makes me lie down in green pastures, he leads me beside quiet waters, he refreshes my soul. He guides me along the right paths for his name's sake. Even though I walk through the darkest valley, I will fear no evil, for you are with me; your rod and your staff, they comfort me. You prepare a table before me in the presence of my enemies. You anoint my head with oil; my cup overflows. Surely your goodness and love will follow me all the days of my life, and I will dwell in the house of the Lord forever.
PSALM 23 NIV

The Bible tells us that the Lord is our shepherd who guides and protects us through all of life's ups and downs. He gives us all the peace and security, goodness and love that we need.

---

*Jesus, I'd be so lost without You!
Thank You for being my good shepherd.*

Give Your Worries and Cares to Jesus

Give all your cares to the Lord and He will give you strength. He will never let those who are right with Him be shaken.
PSALM 55:22 NLV

Jesus is Lord over all of your worries and fears. He promises that those who are right with Him will never be shaken. (You are right with Him when you have chosen Jesus as your Savior.) What are you worried about today? What feels shaky in your life? What are you not feeling sure about? Let the Lord take those things away from you and give you His strength, peace, and power instead. We can trust Him to take care of it all.

Jesus, I don't know why I hold on to worries so often, when You've told me You want to take them away from me and give me strength instead. Please help me give my anxiety to You! I want to trust You more and have more of Your perfect peace and power. Amen.

Avoid Sinful Things

I will set no sinful thing in front of my eyes. I hate the work of those who are not faithful. It will not get hold of me. A sinful heart will be far from me. I will have nothing to do with sin.
PSALM 101:3–4 NLV

The writer of this psalm makes a big promise in this passage. It was easier in his time to make that promise because there were no movies, television shows, smartphones, and social media back then. So we have to be extra careful with what we pay attention to these days because the world is full of sinful things that we can see so easily—and our enemy, the devil, wants to push every sinful thing on us so that we will walk away from following Jesus.

Jesus, I want to make this promise too—I don't want to look at or watch anything that is sinful. I want to keep my mind and heart clean and far away from sin. I need a lot of help with this. Please help me. Amen.

Jesus' Earthly Father, Joseph

[Jesus'] mother, Mary, was engaged to be married to Joseph. But before the marriage took place, while she was still a virgin, she became pregnant through the power of the Holy Spirit. Joseph, to whom she was engaged, was a righteous man and did not want to disgrace her publicly, so he decided to break the engagement quietly. As he considered this, an angel of the Lord appeared to him in a dream. "Joseph, son of David," the angel said, "do not be afraid to take Mary as your wife. For the child within her was conceived by the Holy Spirit. And she will have a son, and you are to name him Jesus, for he will save his people from their sins.". . . When Joseph woke up, he did as the angel of the Lord commanded and took Mary as his wife.
MATTHEW 1:18–21, 24 NLT

Joseph was clearly a good man. He had to have been very upset to learn Mary was pregnant when he knew the child wasn't his. Even so, he didn't want to disgrace Mary publicly. But as he considered what to do, an angel appeared to him to explain everything and give him exact instructions. And Joseph willingly obeyed.

Jesus, help me to listen and obey You, even in unique situations that I don't fully understand. Amen.

Let Jesus Make His Home in Your Heart

Christ will make his home in your hearts as you trust in him. Your roots will grow down into God's love and keep you strong. And may you have the power to understand, as all God's people should, how wide, how long, how high, and how deep his love is. May you experience the love of Christ, though it is too great to understand fully. Then you will be made complete with all the fullness of life and power that comes from God.
EPHESIANS 3:17–19 NLT

The world will tell you all kinds of ways to be a strong young woman, but real, eternal strength comes from Jesus. As you trust in Him, He makes His home in your heart, and you grow stronger every day that you continue to choose Him. Like a tree with good roots, you won't be toppled and broken during the storms of life.

Jesus, help me focus on how incredible and endless Your love for me is! And help me keep on growing stronger every day with You in my heart. Amen.

The Beatitudes

"Blessed are the poor in spirit, for theirs is the kingdom of heaven. Blessed are those who mourn, for they will be comforted. Blessed are the meek, for they will inherit the earth. Blessed are those who hunger and thirst for righteousness, for they will be filled. Blessed are the merciful, for they will be shown mercy. Blessed are the pure in heart, for they will see God. Blessed are the peacemakers, for they will be called children of God. Blessed are those who are persecuted because of righteousness, for theirs is the kingdom of heaven. Blessed are you when people insult you, persecute you and falsely say all kinds of evil against you because of me."

MATTHEW 5:3–11 NIV

Jesus' words in this well-known passage of the Bible called the Beatitudes sound pretty much opposite from what the world tells us will make us happy. Despite the popular messages of our day, wealth, fame, and power are not real sources of blessing. Instead, we are truly blessed and happy when we are humble and do the will of God, loving Him above all and caring for others as He directs us to.

---

*Jesus, please provide me with the blessings
You say are best of all. Amen.*

Worship Jesus

*Make a joyful noise to the L<small>ORD</small>, all the earth!
Serve the L<small>ORD</small> with gladness! Come into his
presence with singing! Know that the L<small>ORD</small>,
he is God! It is he who made us, and we are his;
we are his people, and the sheep of his pasture.
Enter his gates with thanksgiving, and his courts
with praise! Give thanks to him; bless his name!
For the L<small>ORD</small> is good; his steadfast love endures
forever, and his faithfulness to all generations.*
P<small>SALM</small> 100 <small>ESV</small>

With psalms like this and your favorite hymns, worship Jesus! Anytime, anywhere! Even when you need to be quiet, you can focus on praising Jesus in your mind, and immediately you'll be filled with goodness and joy.

Jesus, I am Yours! I want to praise You everywhere I go in everything I do! You are so good and so amazing! Your love is endless, and I'm so grateful. Amen.

Jesus' Cousin John

In those days John the Baptist came preaching in the desert in the country of Judea. He said, "Be sorry for your sins and turn from them! The holy nation of heaven is near." The early preacher Isaiah spoke of this man. He said, "Listen! His voice calls out in the desert! 'Make the way ready for the Lord. Make the road straight for Him!'"
MATTHEW 3:1–3 NLV

Jesus' cousin was John the Baptist. He was an interesting guy! His "clothes were made of camel's hair, and he had a leather belt around his waist. His food was locusts and wild honey" (Matthew 3:4 NIV). He preached to people about the kingdom of heaven and prepared the way for Jesus' ministry. He baptized people but pointed to Jesus, saying, "I baptize with water those who are sorry for their sins and turn from them. The One Who comes after me will baptize you with the Holy Spirit and with fire. He is greater than I. I am not good enough to take off His shoes" (Matthew 3:11 NLV).

Jesus, thank You for teaching me more about You through John the Baptist's ministry. Amen.

Jesus' First Disciples

As Jesus was walking beside the Sea of Galilee, he saw two brothers, Simon called Peter and his brother Andrew. They were casting a net into the lake, for they were fishermen. "Come, follow me," Jesus said, "and I will send you out to fish for people." At once they left their nets and followed him. Going on from there, he saw two other brothers, James son of Zebedee and his brother John. They were in a boat with their father Zebedee, preparing their nets. Jesus called them, and immediately they left the boat and their father and followed him.
MATTHEW 4:18–22 NIV

Jesus chose humble, regular people to call to be His first disciples. They were just fishermen, not royalty, government officials, or wealthy people. Jesus called them to a new type of fishing job—fishing for people who would also want to join in following Jesus. Notice how "at once" and "immediately" these men came to Jesus. We should be inspired to also obey Jesus so quickly when He calls.

Jesus, thank You for the first disciples' example of obedience to You. Thank You for calling humble people to You to be saved. Amen.

New Creation

If anyone is in Christ, he is a new creation.
2 CORINTHIANS 5:17 ESV

When you get weighed down with all the things of this world and all the stress they can cause, you might feel like you need a new start and a new mindset. Does that sound good? When we choose Jesus as Savior, we become new creations, and He then blesses us with endless newness by His grace—for "if we confess our sins, he is faithful and just to forgive us our sins and to cleanse us from all unrighteousness" (1 John 1:9 ESV), and His mercies are new every morning (Lamentations 3:22–23).

Jesus, please help me to remember that I do not belong to this world. I belong to You! I am a new creation because I've chosen You to be my Savior. I want to live with joy and confidence in the facts that You cleanse me from sins when I confess them to You and that You give me new mercy every day. Amen.

Jesus Is the Bread of Life

Jesus said to the people, "For sure, I tell you, it was not Moses who gave you bread from heaven. My Father gives you the true Bread from heaven. The Bread of God is He Who comes down from heaven and gives life to the world." They said to Him, "Sir, give us this Bread all the time." Jesus said to them, "I am the Bread of Life. He who comes to Me will never be hungry. He who puts his trust in Me will never be thirsty."
JOHN 6:32–35 NLV

Do you ever stop to think about how people lived without electricity, indoor plumbing, air-conditioning, or Wi-Fi? How on earth did they do it? It's hard to imagine life without our modern conveniences! But our most basic daily needs for life are food and water, right? So when Jesus calls Himself the "Bread of Life," did He mean that He expects us to believe in Him and then never eat food or drink water again? No. But Jesus does want us to trust in Him as the one who provides for all our needs. *He* is actually our most basic need because He gives us all life and eternal life!

Jesus, thank You for being everything I need. Amen.

Power to Heal

They ran throughout that whole region and carried the sick on mats to wherever they heard he was. And wherever he went—into villages, towns or countryside—they placed the sick in the marketplaces. They begged him to let them touch even the edge of his cloak, and all who touched it were healed.
MARK 6:55–56 NIV

If you or someone you care about is sick, pray. Jesus had the power in Bible times to heal people, and He still has that power today. Sometimes He doesn't heal people here on earth, but we have to remember that forever healing is promised in heaven for all who choose Jesus as the one and only Savior of their sins. There will be no more sickness or death in heaven (Revelation 21:4). Mostly, we should pray for everyone we know to choose Jesus and have forever life too.

Jesus, I pray for You to heal sickness and pain here on earth, and mostly I pray for You to heal people's hearts forever by helping them turn to You as the only Savior from their sins. Amen.

Jesus' Friends Mary and Martha

*Martha welcomed him into her house.
And she had a sister called Mary, who sat at
the Lord's feet and listened to his teaching.*
LUKE 10:38–39 ESV

Mary and Martha were two sisters who loved Jesus and were excited to welcome Him into their home. Martha excelled at planning and preparation and probably wanted everything to be perfect for such a special guest. But Martha got upset with Mary because when Jesus arrived, Mary didn't help her with hosting and serving. Mary simply sat at Jesus' feet to listen to everything He had to say. Both sisters loved Jesus and were showing it in their own unique ways. But Jesus lovingly told Martha that Mary had chosen what was best by simply enjoying His company and listening to His teaching.

---

*Jesus, I want to show my love for You in the
details, like Martha, but I also want to choose
the best way by enjoying simply being with You,
like Mary. Help me to find the right balance. Amen.*

Jesus Calls to Sinners Who Will Repent

Later, as Jesus left the town, he saw a tax collector named Levi sitting at his tax collector's booth. "Follow me and be my disciple," Jesus said to him. So Levi got up, left everything, and followed him. Later, Levi held a banquet in his home with Jesus as the guest of honor. Many of Levi's fellow tax collectors and other guests also ate with them. But the Pharisees and their teachers of religious law complained bitterly to Jesus' disciples, "Why do you eat and drink with such scum?" Jesus answered them, "Healthy people don't need a doctor—sick people do. I have come to call not those who think they are righteous, but those who know they are sinners and need to repent."

LUKE 5:27–32 NLT

Jesus' calling of Levi shows us that people who know they are sinners will choose to follow Jesus. Those who think they do not need forgiveness will not see their need of Him.

Jesus, I know I'm a sinner, and I need Your grace and forgiveness. Thank You for giving it so generously. Amen.

The Best Influencer

We can be sure that we know Him if we obey His teaching. Anyone who says, "I know Him," but does not obey His teaching is a liar. There is no truth in him. But whoever obeys His Word has the love of God made perfect in him. This is the way to know if you belong to Christ. The one who says he belongs to Christ should live the same kind of life Christ lived.
1 JOHN 2:3–6 NLV

You might be impressed by and look up to certain celebrities and influencers, but be sure to choose Jesus as your #1 role model. God the Father sent His Son, Jesus Christ, to earth to be a human being just like all of us and to be our example for living the best kind of life. And how do we follow His example? By reading and studying God's Word to learn more about who God is and how Jesus lived, and by keeping in close relationship with Jesus through prayer and worship.

Jesus, You are my very best influencer and role model. Please help me love learning about You and keep me growing closer to You. Amen.

Jesus Heals a Blind Man

As he went along, he saw a man blind from birth. His disciples asked him, "Rabbi, who sinned, this man or his parents, that he was born blind?" "Neither this man nor his parents sinned," said Jesus, "but this happened so that the works of God might be displayed in him. As long as it is day, we must do the works of him who sent me. Night is coming, when no one can work. While I am in the world, I am the light of the world." After saying this, he spit on the ground, made some mud with the saliva, and put it on the man's eyes. "Go," he told him, "wash in the Pool of Siloam."... So the man went and washed, and came home seeing.

JOHN 9:1–7 NIV

Jesus taught that this man was born blind so that God's work could be shown in him when Jesus healed him and restored his sight. This helps us know that whatever we're struggling with, we can let God's will and work be done and pray for His glory to be shown.

Jesus, thank You for Your healing power. I praise You and want all people to see Your glory! Amen.

Work Hard for Jesus

Do not be lazy but always work hard. Work for the Lord with a heart full of love for Him.
ROMANS 12:11 NLV

What is your work ethic like? Are you willing to work hard? Do you do your best with the gifts and talents God has given you? Having a good work ethic doesn't mean you should never rest or have fun—you absolutely should! But it's so easy to become lazy and have too much rest and fun. Think of the Lord Jesus Himself as the boss overseeing you in any task you do, because ultimately He is! But He's the best kind of boss—full of love and blessing for you as you do the good work you were created for (see Ephesians 2:10).

Jesus, I want to have a work ethic that shows others I work to honor You most of all. Please help me give my best effort and find joy in my work, no matter what it is. You are so good to me, and I'm honored to do my best for You! Amen.

Give with Great Faith

A poor woman whose husband had died came by and gave two very small pieces of money.
MARK 12:42 NLV

One day, Jesus watched many rich people give large offerings to God at the temple. Giving a lot wasn't hard for them because they were so rich that they had plenty of money to share. But then Jesus watched one woman who was very poor and had no husband drop in two coins that were worth less than one cent. And Jesus said to His disciples, "This poor widow has given more money than all the others." But how was that possible? Jesus said, "The rich people put in money they didn't even need because they have so much extra. But the poor widow has nothing extra. She needed every bit of her money to live on, but still she gave it all to God."

Jesus, I want to give to You with great faith just like this widow did, because I trust that You will provide for me no matter what and that Your blessings are greater than anything I could ever gain on my own. Amen.

He Came to Care for Others

*"The Son of Man came not to be cared for.
He came to care for others. He came to give His
life so that many could be bought by His blood
and made free from the punishment of sin."*
MATTHEW 20:28 NLV

Jesus is called the Son of Man, and He is King of all kings and Lord of all lords. But He definitely didn't come to earth in the way we would normally think of royalty—important people who have fancy, expensive everything and servants and staff waiting on their every need. No, Jesus came as a regular person to serve and care for *us*. He cared so much that He even gave His life for us to save us from sin. And once we trust Him as Savior, He asks us to imitate Him by serving and caring for others so that they will want to know Him as Savior too.

---

*Jesus, You are the very best example of
loving and serving others. I want to be as
much like You as I possibly can! Amen.*

Jesus Can Make Our Weak Faith Stronger

"Lord, I have faith. Help my weak faith to be stronger!"
MARK 9:24 NLV

A father was asking Jesus for help for his son, and it was so hard for the man to imagine that Jesus could do what he was asking. The father said to Jesus, "Have mercy on us and help us, if you can." Jesus replied, "What do you mean, 'If I can'? . . . Anything is possible if a person believes" (Mark 9:22–23 NLT). And the father said, "Lord, I have faith. Help my weak faith to be stronger!"

When we pray, we have to remember that Jesus is able to do exactly what we ask and so much more! He may or may not answer the way we hope, but no matter how He responds to our prayers, our main response should be "Lord, I have faith. Help my weak faith to be stronger!"

Jesus, please make my faith in You stronger and stronger every day! Amen.

Lost and Found

*"This younger son. . .wasted all
his money in wild living."*
LUKE 15:13 NLT

Jesus taught about a son who took all of his inheritance from his father and spent it all on a wild and crazy life. After all his money was gone, he was hungry and alone, and the only job he could find was feeding pigs. Then he was ashamed of himself, so he got up and started for home. While he was still a long way off, his father saw him and felt full of love and kindness toward him. He ran to his son and threw his arms around him. The son said, "Father, I have sinned against both heaven and you, and I am no longer worthy of being called your son" (Luke 15:18–19 NLT). But the father said to his workmen, "We must celebrate with a feast, for this son of mine was dead and has now returned to life. He was lost, but now he is found" (Luke 15:23–24 NLT).

Jesus, like You taught in this parable, help me to realize my mistakes, own them, apologize for them, and turn away from them and back to Your good ways. Thank You for Your love and mercy. Amen.

Physically and Spiritually

[Jesus said:] "Is it easier to say to the paralyzed man 'Your sins are forgiven,' or 'Stand up, pick up your mat, and walk'? So I will prove to you that the Son of Man has the authority on earth to forgive sins." Then Jesus turned to the paralyzed man and said, "Stand up, pick up your mat, and go home!" And the man jumped up, grabbed his mat, and walked out through the stunned onlookers. They were all amazed and praised God, exclaiming, "We've never seen anything like this before!"

MARK 2:9–12 NLT

Read this whole account in Mark 2, and you'll see that this paralyzed man had been lowered into the room where Jesus was through a hole in the roof! There were so many people crowded in to listen to Jesus teach that day that there was no other way to reach Him. Jesus was impressed by their faith, and through this experience, He taught those listening that He has the power to heal both physically and spiritually. Only the one true God can forgive sins, and Jesus was proving that He is one with God.

Jesus, Your power, authority, mercy, and love are amazing! Amen.

Yes, You Might Be Insulted

If you are insulted because you bear the name of Christ, you will be blessed, for the glorious Spirit of God rests upon you.
1 PETER 4:14 NLT

Choosing Jesus means you may be insulted if you're doing your best to follow Him and obey God's Word. What's cool and popular in the world is often so opposite of what God's Word says is good and right. And when you don't go along with what's cool and popular, there's a good chance someone will make fun of you. That's not easy to deal with, but you can handle it. You are strong and brave because of the power of Jesus in you. He promises to bless you, and His Holy Spirit never, ever leaves you.

Jesus, I'll keep on choosing You and following You and am happy to be called a Christian no matter what anyone else says about me. You make me strong and brave, and You fill my life with blessings. Amen.

With Jesus, You Are Always Stronger

The One Who lives in you is stronger than the one who is in the world.
1 JOHN 4:4 NLV

Our enemy, the devil, is stirring up all kinds of evil in this world. And you will be under attack from him and from the power of sin in all sorts of ways—through someone else's unkind words or actions, through stressful times for your family, through painful times of loss, through sickness, and so on. You can probably make a list right now, unfortunately. But no matter how strong the enemy and his evil seem, the devil is never stronger than the power of God in you through the Holy Spirit—all because you have chosen Jesus as your Savior.

Jesus, sometimes I forget the truth that You are always stronger than any evil attack against me, any hard thing I'm going through. Please remind me and fill me with Your strength and power through the Holy Spirit. Amen.

Humble Servant Leader

After Jesus had washed his disciples' feet. . . he said: Do you understand what I have done? You call me your teacher and Lord, and you should, because that is who I am. And if your Lord and teacher has washed your feet, you should do the same for each other. I have set the example, and you should do for each other exactly what I have done for you. I tell you for certain that servants are not greater than their master, and messengers are not greater than the one who sent them. You know these things, and God will bless you, if you do them.
JOHN 13:12–17 CEV

Jesus is King of kings and Lord of lords. Everyone on earth will bow down to Him one day. At the same time, He is truly a humble servant leader. He showed an example of that when He washed His disciples' feet. And He taught that they should do the same and that they would be blessed for being humble servants of each other. That message was not just for the disciples; it's for us too.

Jesus, thank You for showing us how to be humble and have compassion, how to serve and love others. I want to be like You and treat others like You do. Amen.

Our Perfect Home Forever

"Do not let your hearts be troubled. You believe in God; believe also in me. My Father's house has many rooms; if that were not so, would I have told you that I am going there to prepare a place for you? And if I go and prepare a place for you, I will come back and take you to be with me that you also may be where I am. You know the way to the place where I am going."
JOHN 14:1–4 NIV

Our perfect forever home is waiting for us in heaven—in God's house! Jesus talked about its many rooms. Those rooms will be far cooler than anything we can imagine! We can talk to Jesus anytime and tell Him what we hope heaven will be like, and then we can tell Him that we simply trust it will be the very best because we will live with Him there.

Jesus, I believe that heaven will be awesome! I'm so thankful You have saved me from my sin so that I get to spend forever at home with You! Amen.

Super Generous Forgiveness

Peter came to Jesus and asked, "Lord, how many times shall I forgive my brother or sister who sins against me? Up to seven times?" Jesus answered, "I tell you, not seven times, but seventy-seven times."
MATTHEW 18:21–22 NIV

Jesus is not stingy or cheap with forgiveness. He's super generous about it, and He taught us to be too. When His disciple Peter asked how many times he should forgive someone sinning against him, Jesus answered that whatever amount we first think is right, we should go way above and beyond that amount—because Jesus goes way above and beyond at loving and forgiving us! That's an incredible blessing, and we should want to share that blessing.

Jesus, please help me to do my best at forgiving others in over-the-top, above-and-beyond kinds of ways like You forgive me. Amen.

Jesus and Lazarus

They took away the stone. Then Jesus looked up and said, "Father, I thank you that you have heard me. I knew that you always hear me, but I said this for the benefit of the people standing here, that they may believe that you sent me." When he had said this, Jesus called in a loud voice, "Lazarus, come out!" The dead man came out, his hands and feet wrapped with strips of linen, and a cloth around his face. Jesus said to them, "Take off the grave clothes and let him go."
JOHN 11:41–44 NIV

Jesus completely amazed the people when He healed His friend Lazarus, who had been dead for four days. But Jesus did this to help people believe in Him as God and to choose Him as Savior and receive forgiveness of sins and eternal life beyond this world. He had said this to Martha just before He called her brother Lazarus out of the tomb: "I am the resurrection and the life. The one who believes in me will live, even though they die; and whoever lives by believing in me will never die. Do you believe this?" (John 11:25–26 NIV).

Jesus, yes, I believe You are the resurrection and the life! Amen.

Before You Ask

[Jesus said:] "Your Father knows what you need before you ask him."
MATTHEW 6:8 ESV

If Jesus taught that your heavenly Father knows what you need before you even ask Him, you might say, "Why should I pray at all? God already knows!" And the answer is, "Because God loves you that much, that's why!" He wants a close relationship with you that much. He wants to hear from you even though He already knows everything about you and everything you need!

Really think about that for a minute—the God of the whole universe wants to be in close relationship with you. That's incredible! The fact that He already knows everything about you plus everything about *everything* is a reason to want to talk to Him all the more, never a reason to think you don't need to bother.

Jesus, thank You for teaching me about God's great love for me. Amen.

Childlike Faith

[Jesus] said to them, "Let the children come to me. Don't stop them! For the Kingdom of God belongs to those who are like these children. I tell you the truth, anyone who doesn't receive the Kingdom of God like a child will never enter it."
MARK 10:14–15 NLT

As you look to the future, what are the things you're looking forward to about not being a teen anymore? What are the things you will miss? It's fun to hold on to childish youth in some ways, although it's good (and necessary) to grow and mature. It's great, then, that Jesus tells us we should always be childlike in the way we have a relationship with Him. When we're young, we're pretty carefree, eager, and enthusiastic. We have great love for and faith in our parents or caretakers. And in that same kind of way, Jesus wants us to remain like children forever—trusting in Him completely to provide for every need and eagerly enjoy His great love for us.

Jesus, even as I'm maturing, help me to always have childlike, enthusiastic love, joy, and faith in You. Amen.

Plans and Steps

*We can make our plans, but the
Lord determines our steps.*
PROVERBS 16:9 NLT

It's good to make goals and go after them, but as we do so, we must ask Jesus what His will is and be willing to change our plans if He directs us to. He will determine each of our steps—and even if it's hard sometimes, we need to willingly accept that. Sometimes His steps for us will match exactly what we hoped for, and sometimes He might want to teach us something totally different from what we wanted. But when we humbly follow Jesus anywhere He says to go, He is going to lead us along the very best paths and plans for our lives.

---

*Jesus, please change my plans as You see fit.
Help me to humbly trust and follow You because
I love You and I know You love me. Amen.*

Detailed Love

[Jesus said:] "Are not two small birds sold for a very small piece of money? And yet not one of the birds falls to the earth without your Father knowing it. God knows how many hairs you have on your head. So do not be afraid. You are more important than many small birds."
MATTHEW 10:29–31 NLV

Jesus taught that there is no one who knows and loves you like your heavenly Father does. Your family and friends might know a lot of details about you, but not even the closest one of them knows how many hairs are on your head. God cares about everything in His creation, even the tiniest of birds, but He knows and loves people most of all—and that definitely includes you!

Jesus, thank You for teaching me that God knows me even better than I know myself and loves me like crazy. Help me to focus on that truth and never forget it! Amen.

A Rich Man and Jesus

"Good Teacher, what must I do to inherit eternal life?"... "I've obeyed all these commandments since I was young." Looking at the man, Jesus felt genuine love for him. "There is still one thing you haven't done," he told him. "Go and sell all your possessions and give the money to the poor, and you will have treasure in heaven. Then come, follow me." At this the man's face fell, and he went away sad, for he had many possessions. Jesus looked around and said to his disciples, "How hard it is for the rich to enter the Kingdom of God!"
MARK 10:17, 20–23 NLT

This rich man loved to obey God's commandments and had a desire to know Jesus, but he wasn't willing to truly follow, obey, and believe Jesus because he showed he wanted to hold on to his wealth, not give it up when Jesus asked. If we truly love Jesus as our Savior, we give up anything we have if Jesus asks us because we know that no possession or wealth here on earth compares to the love and salvation He offers.

Jesus, help me to always be willing to give up everything and obey You no matter what. Amen.

No Fear

[Jesus said:] "Don't be afraid of those who threaten you. For the time is coming when everything that is covered will be revealed, and all that is secret will be made known to all. . . . Don't be afraid of those who want to kill your body; they cannot touch your soul. Fear only God, who can destroy both soul and body in hell."
MATTHEW 10:26, 28 NLT

Jesus taught us to have no fear. Evil people and evil plans will be uncovered eventually. Above all, God sees and will bring consequences and justice. Keep praying to Him to do that and for wisdom about how to be strong against enemies, for protection, and for courage!

Jesus, remind me every day that I don't need to be afraid of anyone. You see and know all; You protect and provide; and You will make everything right in Your perfect timing. I fear and respect You alone. You are my Savior, and I know how much You love me. Amen.

So Much More

Simon said to Him, "Teacher, we have worked all night and we have caught nothing. But because You told me to, I will let the net down." When they had done this, they caught so many fish, their net started to break. They called to their friends working in the other boat to come and help them. They came and both boats were so full of fish they began to sink.
LUKE 5:5–7 NLV

Jesus' disciples had just spent the whole night fishing and had caught nothing, but Jesus only had to say the words. . . and they suddenly caught loads of fish—enough to tear their nets and sink their boats! Never forget that Jesus is able to bless you with so much more than you expect. Keep learning about Him, trusting Him, praising Him, waiting on His perfect timing, and asking Him for everything you need. He just might provide so much more than you ever dreamed possible!

Jesus, help me to remember how You love to bless people—including me— in above-and-beyond kinds of ways! Amen.

Match Your Words and Actions

*Let's not merely say that we love each other;
let us show the truth by our actions.*
1 JOHN 3:18 NLT

Do you ever observe people saying nice things but then doing nasty things? We're all guilty of that sometimes, and we need to be careful that we live honest lives—matching what we say with what we do. What Jesus says *always* matches what He does. His words are *always* true. He didn't just say He loves us; He proved His great love for all people with action. Romans 5:8 (NLV) says, "God showed His love to us. While we were still sinners, Christ died for us."

Jesus, I want to keep on learning from Your love, Your words, and Your actions. Please help my life to be a lot like Yours. I want to love not just in words but in everything I do.

Watch Out!

[Jesus said:] Watch out for false prophets! They dress up like sheep, but inside they are wolves who have come to attack you. You can tell what they are by what they do.... You can tell who the false prophets are by their deeds.
MATTHEW 7:15–16, 20 CEV

Jesus warned strongly against false prophets and teachers for good reason. There are some really confusing differences among churches and people who call themselves Christians. Some differences are no big deal because they're just a matter of traditions and preferences. But some differences result from people going against the Word of God. Second Corinthians 11:13 (CEV) says these false teachers "only pretend to be apostles of Christ." Jesus is not surprised by these false teachers and churches, so we don't have to be afraid. If we keep ourselves strongly dependent on Jesus and the Bible through the Holy Spirit, He will help us distinguish the false teachers and churches from those who truly know, love, and serve Him and preach the whole Word of God.

Jesus, I want to hear what You want to teach me, straight from Your Word and Your leading! Amen.

Drastic Change

Saul was still breathing out murderous threats against the Lord's disciples. . . . As he neared Damascus on his journey, suddenly a light from heaven flashed around him. He fell to the ground and heard a voice say to him, "Saul, Saul, why do you persecute me?"
ACTS 9:1, 3–4 NIV

Saul had a dramatic experience when Jesus stopped him in his tracks and completely turned his life around. He went from hating and hunting down Christians to being Jesus' chosen instrument to spread His truth and love. (Read on in Acts 9 to get the full story.) It's truly miraculous and amazing what Jesus can do to change people drastically. Don't forget how Jesus can keep working in your life to turn around any difficult situation, and He can change the heart of any person you know who still needs to choose Him as Savior. So keep praying and trusting!

Lord, I believe You still work in dramatic, miraculous ways today to change people and help them choose You. Amen.

Too Wonderful to Be Measured

I want you to know all about Christ's love, although it is too wonderful to be measured. Then your lives will be filled with all that God is. I pray that Christ Jesus and the church will forever bring praise to God. His power at work in us can do far more than we dare ask or imagine.
EPHESIANS 3:19–21 CEV

The love of Jesus is so wonderful, so above and beyond, so much bigger than anything that anyone can ever measure or even possibly imagine, and He is able to do so much more than our very best hopes and dreams! As you pray and ask for His blessings and help in every area of your life, think about how great His love for you is and how His plans for your life are always the best.

Jesus, thank You for Your endless, immeasurable, awesome love and power in my life! Amen.

Give Your Way to Jesus

Be happy in the Lord. And He will give you the desires of your heart. Give your way over to the Lord. Trust in Him also. And He will do it. He will make your being right and good show as the light, and your wise actions as the noon day. Rest in the Lord and be willing to wait for Him.
PSALM 37:4–7 NLV

What does it mean to "Give your way over to the Lord"? It means you say, "I don't want my own way, Jesus. I want Your way instead. Guide me on the good and right paths that You have planned for me." Ask Jesus to help you rest in Him and let your joy come from trusting Him. He gave you your life, and you can let Him lead it. He wants to bless you in the best kind of ways, always.

Jesus, help me to want Your way in my life. I want all my happiness and joy to come from following You, resting in You, and waiting on You! Amen.

A Solitary Place to Pray

Very early in the morning, while it was still dark, Jesus got up, left the house and went off to a solitary place, where he prayed. Simon and his companions went to look for him, and when they found him, they exclaimed: "Everyone is looking for you!"

MARK 1:35–37 NIV

Even when Jesus had many things to do and many people wanting to see Him, hear Him, learn from Him, and be healed by Him, He took time to get away and pray. We need to remember this lesson daily—that if even Jesus, who was sinless and perfect, needed alone time to rest away from other people and spend time in prayer, how much more do we need that kind of time?

Jesus, help me to remember Your example of quiet, alone time and prayer. I don't want other responsibilities to get in the way of making You my priority. Help me to balance and prioritize my life well, with You first. Amen.

The Spirit Is Willing, but the Body Is Weak

[Jesus said:] "Watch and pray so that you will not be tempted. Man's spirit is willing, but the body does not have the power to do it."
MATTHEW 26:41 NLV

Sometimes we have good intentions to do a good job with something, and then we just don't follow through. Can you relate? Do you ever plan to study really well for an upcoming test, but then find yourself quickly cramming the night before? Do you ever plan to have regular time with Jesus, but you keep letting everything else in your life take priority over Him?

We are human, and we have struggles and temptations that keep us from doing the good things we should do and we intend to do. That's why we need to pray for help. We need to tell Jesus, "I can't do this on my own! Because of sin, I'm tempted to mess up all the time! I need Your great big power working in me to overcome this temptation."

Jesus, I can't do anything good without You! Please help me with everything! Amen.

Zacchaeus and Jesus

He was seeking to see who Jesus was.
LUKE 19:3 ESV

Zacchaeus was a tax collector known for cheating and taking way too much of other people's money. But Zacchaeus was curious about Jesus and wanted to see Him as He traveled through Jericho. He wasn't very tall, so he ran ahead of where Jesus would walk and climbed a tree. Soon Jesus was near, and when He reached that tree, He stopped and spotted Zacchaeus. He called him by name and said, "Come down right away. I'm going to your house today." Zacchaeus climbed down immediately and welcomed Jesus to his home. As Zacchaeus spent time with Jesus, he was sorry for his sins. He wanted to give back to people all the money he had cheated them out of plus four times more.

Jesus, I'm thankful for the example of Zacchaeus, who was determined to get close to You and then admitted his sins and wanted to make things right. I want to be a lot like Zacchaeus. Amen.

Choose Real Love and Joy

"I have loved you even as the Father has loved me. Remain in my love. When you obey my commandments, you remain in my love, just as I obey my Father's commandments and remain in his love. I have told you these things so that you will be filled with my joy. Yes, your joy will overflow! This is my commandment: Love each other in the same way I have loved you."
JOHN 15:9–12 NLT

The world around us gives all kinds of bad ideas of what love and joy are. But Jesus tells us in John 15 how to have *real* love and joy. When we obey Jesus the way He obeyed God, we stay close to God. And because God is love (see 1 John 4:8), our whole life is lived in love. When we live in real love, we can't help but be full of real joy because we are living exactly the way God intended when He created us!

Jesus, I want to live in Your real love and be full of the real joy that comes only from choosing You! Amen.

Different Gifts from the Same God

There are different kinds of spiritual gifts, but they all come from the same Spirit. There are different ways to serve the same Lord, and we can each do different things. Yet the same God works in all of us and helps us in everything we do.
1 CORINTHIANS 12:4–6 CEV

Our world would be so dull if everyone had the same personalities, abilities, and talents! The Bible talks about how the Holy Spirit gives different gifts to each of His people, different ways to serve Jesus, different ways to help one another. God has blessed us all with unique talents and individual abilities to do what He asks us to do. It's so important to never compare and expect other Christians to be exactly like us. God purposefully made us different, with tasks designed specifically for us. We can let Him show us what they are and then do them for His glory!

Jesus, thank You for my unique gifts. Help me to know how and when to use them like You want me to. Amen.

Watch Out for Those Who Leave Jesus Out

Be careful that no one changes your mind and faith by much learning and big sounding ideas. Those things are what men dream up. They are always trying to make new religions. These leave out Christ. For Christ is not only God-like, He is God in human flesh. When you have Christ, you are complete. He is the head over all leaders and powers. When you became a Christian, you were set free from the sinful things of the world.
COLOSSIANS 2:8–11 NLV

Any teaching of this world about faith that excludes Jesus is false religion, a waste of time. Our faith in Jesus depends on the fact that He alone is the risen Savior who conquered death and paid the price for our sin. First Corinthians 15:17, 19–20 (CEV) says, "Unless Christ was raised to life, your faith is useless, and you are still living in your sins. . . . If our hope in Christ is good only for this life, we are worse off than anyone else. But Christ has been raised to life!"

Jesus, You are alive, and I praise You! You alone are the one true risen Savior; You alone are worthy of faith! Help me watch for and avoid any teaching that leaves You out! Amen.

Nathanael and Jesus

As they approached, Jesus said, "Now here is a genuine son of Israel—a man of complete integrity." "How do you know about me?" Nathanael asked. Jesus replied, "I could see you under the fig tree before Philip found you." Then Nathanael exclaimed, "Rabbi, you are the Son of God—the King of Israel!" Jesus asked him, Do you believe this just because I told you I had seen you under the fig tree? You will see greater things than this."
JOHN 1:47–50 NLT

Jesus described Nathanael as a man of complete integrity. What a compliment from the only one who knows everything! Still, Nathanael needed to change his life to love and follow Jesus, just like we all do! It's wonderful to be a good and kind person, but even the most moral and nicest people still need to choose Jesus as Savior.

Jesus, help me remind myself and show others that being kind and full of integrity is wonderful, but even the best-behaved people still need to choose You as Savior. Amen.

When You Feel Like Quitting

Christ gives me the strength to face anything.
PHILIPPIANS 4:13 CEV

Have you ever just wanted to immediately quit something you're involved in? We've all been there. But when we do finish something without quitting in the middle of it, we can usually look back and see how Jesus was giving us just what we needed to take things one day at a time. And hopefully, we can see how He used that time to grow us into better, stronger people because we pushed through with commitment and endurance instead of giving up. In any hard situation, be sure to call on Jesus for help; then trust in Him and wait on Him. He will either help you walk through it day by day until it's over or help you find a wise way out ASAP.

---

*Jesus, please help me when I want to
quit in the middle of hard circumstances.
Please give me endurance, strength, courage,
and wisdom. And please help me find joy
in the midst of the struggle too. Amen.*

Gather

[Jesus said:] "For where two or three are gathered together in My name, there I am with them."
MATTHEW 18:20 NLV

Do you have friends and/or family members with whom you share needs, concerns, and worries? Do you also spend time praying together about those things? If not, start a regular prayer time with the people you love. No matter where you are, offer to pray for your friends and ask them to pray for you too. Find smart ways and times to share needs and join together in prayer. Prayer is always powerful, and gathering together to support each other with prayer brings about more of its benefits and power in your lives.

Jesus, thank You that we can pray to You anytime, anywhere! Thank You for family and friends and the times when we gather so we can all talk to You together. These times are so encouraging as we focus on You and bring our praise and needs to You. Amen.

Jesus Did All the Work

You cannot make God accept you because of something you do. God accepts sinners only because they have faith in him.
ROMANS 4:5 CEV

We cannot do any work or good deed to save us from our sin and get us to heaven. Imagine how exhausting trying to work for our salvation would be, how anxious we'd feel as we wondered if we were ever doing a good enough job! Thankfully, our salvation is a gift from God that we receive from Him because of our faith. We believe that God provided Jesus to do the work on the cross to pay the price for our sins, and we believe that Jesus died on the cross and rose again. We believe that the only way to be made right with God is through Jesus Christ. We admit our sin and ask God to forgive us for it, and we let Jesus be Lord over our lives and do our best to obey Him and follow His ways, which we learn from the Bible and guidance of the Holy Spirit.

---

*Jesus, You did all the work to save me.
I am beyond grateful, and I want to live all
my life to honor and praise You. Amen.*

Jesus Is the Great High Priest

We have a great high priest, who has gone into heaven, and he is Jesus the Son of God. This is why we must hold on to what we have said about him. Jesus understands every weakness of ours, because he was tempted in every way that we are. But he did not sin! So whenever we are in need, we should come bravely before the throne of our merciful God. There we will be treated with undeserved grace, and we will find help.
HEBREWS 4:14–16 CEV

It can be super intimidating to talk to well-known people and important leaders. So it's pretty cool that God's Word tells us that Jesus made the way for us to go to God, who is the King of kings, with total trust and confidence! We can even call Him "Abba" (Romans 8:15), which is a term like "Daddy"—that's how close of a relationship we can have with one true Almighty God because of Jesus.

Jesus, I'm so grateful that because I've chosen You as Savior, You've brought me into close relationship with Almighty God. Amazing! Amen.

Jesus Calls Us Out of Darkness

He called you out of the darkness into his wonderful light.
1 PETER 2:9 NLT

It's so important to let the light that is in us because of Jesus shine so brightly that others might leave the darkness and come to know Him too. We need to show others that we are different from the dark world around us. Ephesians 4:17–24 (CEV) states it with strong, straightforward words: "Stop living like stupid, godless people. Their minds are in the dark, and they are stubborn and ignorant and have missed out on the life that comes from God. They no longer have any feelings about what is right, and they are so greedy they do all kinds of indecent things. But this isn't what you were taught about Jesus Christ. He is the truth, and you heard about him and learned about him. You were told that your foolish desires will destroy you and that you must give up your old way of life with all its bad habits. Let the Spirit change your way of thinking and make you into a new person."

Jesus, please help me to turn from anything that is of the darkness and live in Your wonderful light. Amen.

Make Peace, Not Drama

[Jesus said:] God blesses those people who make peace.
MATTHEW 5:9 CEV

Some people seem to love drama and love to stir it up for any reason. But that's not right. We shouldn't love being in conflict and competition with others. Instead, we should always want good and peaceful relationships. We should encourage each other, forgive each other generously, and stop gossiping or causing fights. Jesus said God blesses those who make peace, and you can't make anything without some work. It takes some working out of disagreements and trouble to make peace sometimes; it's not just going along with anything to try to keep everyone happy and drama-free. We need so much wisdom to know how to do this right. Fortunately, the Bible promises us that God loves to give us wisdom (see James 1:5). Jesus wants to help us with our problems—we just have to keep on asking and listening to Him!

---

*Jesus, please help me to make peace,
not drama, in all my situations and
relationships with other people. Amen.*

Keep On Trusting

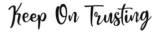

Even when I am afraid, I keep on trusting you. I praise your promises! I trust you and am not afraid. No one can harm me.
PSALM 56:3–4 CEV

What good is it if one time we just said we trusted in Jesus, and that was it? Just one time isn't right. We have to keep trusting even when we're afraid, confused, angry, and heartbroken—no matter what is going on in our lives! We must choose to trust in Jesus again and again each day, knowing we face new challenges and enemies and realizing that we need to focus on His perfect promises every day to guide us and protect us.

Jesus, again today, I choose to trust You! I want this to be my prayer every day! Only You can lead me with the light that leads to life. Amen.

When Jesus Was Tempted

Then Jesus was led by the Spirit into the wilderness to be tempted there by the devil. For forty days and forty nights he fasted and became very hungry. During that time the devil came.
MATTHEW 4:1–3 NLT

When we read the whole account of Jesus' temptation by Satan in Matthew 4, we learn how to deal with similar temptation. It shows us how dangerous Satan can be. He will do anything to try to destroy us and make us turn away from obeying God. He knows scripture too, and he might even twist it to try to confuse us and take it out of context to get us to sin. Lots of people in our world also work in those same ways to try to turn us away from Jesus. We have to keep asking Jesus for protection, wisdom, and strength to stand up against Satan's lies and ploys. And ultimately we must tell him the same thing Jesus told him: "Get out of here, Satan. . . . For the Scriptures say, 'You must worship the LORD your God and serve only him'" (Matthew 4:10 NLT).

Jesus, help me to be strong against Satan's lies and ploys like You were. I worship and serve You alone! Amen.

Because You Are Loved and Chosen

God loves you and has chosen you as his own special people. So be gentle, kind, humble, meek, and patient. Put up with each other, and forgive anyone who does you wrong, just as Christ has forgiven you. Love is more important than anything else. It is what ties everything completely together. Each one of you is part of the body of Christ, and you were chosen to live together in peace. So let the peace that comes from Christ control your thoughts. And be grateful.
COLOSSIANS 3:12–15 CEV

Life is full of messes and mistakes that we all are guilty of making sometimes. Since we are God's loved and chosen people because we've chosen Jesus as Savior, we must remember this scripture and let love, gentleness, kindness, humility, meekness, patience, gratitude, and the peace that comes from Jesus control our minds, hearts, and actions toward others—just like we need others to do the same for us.

Jesus, please fill me with all the peace and goodness that come from You, and help me share it with others generously. Amen.

Care Like Jesus

Jesus cured many people of their diseases, illnesses, and evil spirits, and he restored sight to many who were blind. Then he told John's disciples, "Go back to John and tell him what you have seen and heard— the blind see, the lame walk, those with leprosy are cured, the deaf hear, the dead are raised to life, and the Good News is being preached to the poor."
LUKE 7:21–22 NLT

Jesus loved and cared for people like no other human ever has or ever will. He healed and provided for the sick and needy. He reached out to the lonely and unwanted. He boldly taught the truth and showed people the one and only way to God in heaven. And if we are true followers of Jesus, we will do our best at these things too! Keep asking Jesus how He wants you to be like Him, care for the needs of others, and help spread His truth.

Jesus, like You, I want to truly love and reach out to and care for people. Please help me. Amen.

Straight Paths

Trust in the Lord with all your heart, and do not trust in your own understanding. Agree with Him in all your ways, and He will make your paths straight. Do not be wise in your own eyes. Fear the Lord and turn away from what is sinful.
PROVERBS 3:5–7 NLV

Even though so many messages and themes you hear these days tell you to trust your heart and follow your dreams, that's not always the best advice. Before you do, make sure your heart and your dreams match with what Jesus wants for you. Too often we're tempted and motivated by what is sinful and bad for us. So His Word tells us to trust Him with all our hearts and not to lean on our own understanding. We need to stay close to Him through reading His Word, praying, worshipping Him, and serving Him. We can trust Him to make straight paths for our dreams when they match up with His perfect plans for our lives.

Jesus, please help me agree with You in all my ways. I want to trust in You more than myself. Amen.

With Great Love and Gratitude

When a sinful woman in that town found out that Jesus was there, she bought an expensive bottle of perfume. Then she came and stood behind Jesus. She cried and started washing his feet with her tears and drying them with her hair. The woman kissed his feet and poured the perfume on them.
LUKE 7:37–38 CEV

This woman had done a lot of bad things in her life, but she chose to trust Jesus as her Savior to forgive her sins. And she wanted to show Jesus her great gratitude in a special kind of way. The proud Pharisees were angry that Jesus allowed this woman to act this way toward Him, but Jesus said, "I tell you that all her sins are forgiven, and that is why she has shown great love. But anyone who has been forgiven for only a little will show only a little love" (Luke 7:47 CEV).

Jesus, thank You for the example of the woman who washed Your feet with her tears and gave You expensive perfume. I want to show my love and gratitude for You as my Savior in generous and special ways too! Amen.

Jesus Sees It All

*The eyes of the Lord are in every place,
watching the bad and the good.*
PROVERBS 15:3 NLV

"No one can hide from God. His eyes see everything we do. We must give an answer to God for what we have done," says Hebrews 4:13 (NLV). And Job 28:24 (NLV) says, "He looks to the ends of the earth, and sees everything under the heavens." For people who make a lot of bad choices, these verses might seem annoying, oppressive, or even scary, but for those who choose Jesus as Savior and want to follow and obey Him, they are hopeful and encouraging. Jesus wants you to be saved and obey His good ways because He loves you and wants what's best for you. When you trust that He is always watching out for you, you can have peace and confidence, knowing He's able to guide you and help you in every moment.

---

*Jesus, I know You are always watching
me, and that's such a gift and blessing.
Thank You for caring so much about me! Amen.*

Choose Jesus Every Morning

Each morning let me learn more about your love because I trust you. I come to you in prayer, asking for your guidance. Please rescue me from my enemies, LORD! I come to you for safety. You are my God. Show me what you want me to do, and let your gentle Spirit lead me in the right path.
PSALM 143:8–10 CEV

Spend some time with Jesus every morning. Ask the Lord to tell you about His unfailing love each new day. Ask Him to show you how to make good choices and how to avoid bad choices—where you *shouldn't* go in your day. Let Him teach you how to do His will and lead you on the right path.

Jesus, I want to begin my days with You. Please lead me and help me to follow the good things You have planned for me. Amen.

Choose Jesus Every Night

Your love means more than life to me, and I praise you. As long as I live, I will pray to you. I will sing joyful praises and be filled with excitement like a guest at a banquet. I think about you, God, before I go to sleep, and my thoughts turn to you during the night. You have helped me, and I sing happy songs in the shadow of your wings.
PSALM 63:3–7 CEV

Spend time with Jesus every night too. Actually, you can spend time with Jesus any time of the day! It's important to regularly praise Him and pray to Him, listen to Him and learn from Him—especially through reading the Bible, His Word.

Jesus, please help me to remember that any time of day or night is a good time to spend with You. I'm so glad that You are always right here with me. Amen.

Let Jesus Make a Lot from a Little

"There's a young boy here with five barley loaves and two fish. But what good is that with this huge crowd?" "Tell everyone to sit down," Jesus said. So they all sat down on the grassy slopes. (The men alone numbered about 5,000.) . . . After everyone was full, Jesus told his disciples, "Now gather the leftovers, so that nothing is wasted." So they picked up the pieces and filled twelve baskets with scraps left by the people who had eaten.
JOHN 6:8–10, 12–13 NLT

Jesus did an amazing thing when He took that little lunch and fed a huge crowd of people with many basketfuls left over. Think about how many of those people must have believed in Jesus that day after seeing such a stunning miracle. Let this inspire you to be faithful even in the smallest things Jesus asks you to do and give. Who knows how He will bless and show you miracles because of your obedience and generosity?

Jesus, I want to be faithful to You even in the little things. Please take what I can give and turn it into something so much bigger for Your glory! Amen.

Love Your Enemies

"I say, love your enemies! Pray for those who persecute you! In that way, you will be acting as true children of your Father in heaven. For he gives his sunlight to both the evil and the good, and he sends rain on the just and the unjust alike. If you love only those who love you, what reward is there for that?"
MATTHEW 5:44–46 NLT

Love your enemies and pray for them, even though that is extremely hard to do. Why? Because Jesus said so. He will help us, and when we choose to love and pray for our enemies like Jesus taught, we are acting like true children of God. That's a big deal!

Jesus, it's really hard to pray for people who treat me terribly! But I want to do my best with Your help because I love You and want to obey You. It's only with Your grace and power that I can do this. I trust You to help me, and I pray for these people right now. Amen.

Build on Jesus

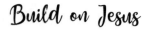

"Everyone who hears these words of mine and puts them into practice is like a wise man who built his house on the rock. The rain came down, the streams rose, and the winds blew and beat against that house; yet it did not fall, because it had its foundation on the rock. But everyone who hears these words of mine and does not put them into practice is like a foolish man who built his house on sand. The rain came down, the streams rose, and the winds blew and beat against that house, and it fell with a great crash."
MATTHEW 7:24–27 NIV

Jesus taught that it matters what we build our lives on. He contrasted people who heard His teaching and listened and obeyed it with people who heard it but did nothing. Those who obey Jesus are built up strong for whatever life brings their way; those who ignore Jesus are easily washed away. What are you building on?

Jesus, I'm building on You! Please strengthen me with great faith as I depend on You to be my rock in every kind of weather! Amen.

Jesus' Glorious Return

We are filled with hope, as we wait for the glorious return of our great God and Savior Jesus Christ. He gave himself to rescue us from everything evil and to make our hearts pure.
TITUS 2:13–14 CEV

Jesus will come back someday, and the Bible tells us that we should always be filled with hope, watching and waiting for His return. (See also Matthew 25:13, Luke 21:25–28, and Hebrews 9:28.) It will be unlike anything any person has ever experienced, but it will be wonderful for everyone who has chosen to trust Jesus. Mark 13:24–27 (CEV) says: "'The sun will become dark, and the moon will no longer shine. The stars will fall, and the powers in the sky will be shaken.' Then the Son of Man will be seen coming in the clouds with great power and glory. He will send his angels to gather his chosen ones from all over the earth."

Jesus, I'm watching and waiting for You to return and gather Your people, including me! I love You and trust You because I have chosen You, so I am one of Your chosen. Amen.

Good Soil, Strong Roots

"A farmer went out to plant his seed."
LUKE 8:5 NLT

Jesus told a parable to help us learn more about having strong roots, and then He explained the parable this way: "The seed is God's word. The seeds that fell on the footpath represent those who hear the message, only to have the devil come and take it away from their hearts and prevent them from believing and being saved. The seeds on the rocky soil represent those who hear the message and receive it with joy. But since they don't have deep roots, they believe for a while, then they fall away when they face temptation. The seeds that fell among the thorns represent those who hear the message, but all too quickly the message is crowded out by the cares and riches and pleasures of this life. And so they never grow into maturity. And the seeds that fell on the good soil represent honest, good-hearted people who hear God's word, cling to it, and patiently produce a huge harvest" (Luke 8:11–15 NLT).

Jesus, help me to be that last kind of seed—a person growing in good soil with roots that are strong in You! Amen.

Teamwork and Unity

"May they experience such perfect unity that the world will know that you sent me and that you love them as much as you love me."
JOHN 17:23 NLT

Jesus wanted all of His followers to have good teamwork. He prayed for unity—that all of His followers throughout all of time would be one team with God, the Father, and Jesus, the Son, working together to share God's love and help more and more people believe in Jesus. You can read Jesus' prayer in John 17:20–21, 23 (NLT): "I am praying not only for these disciples but also for all who will ever believe in me through their message. I pray that they will all be one, just as you and I are one—as you are in me, Father, and I am in you. And may they be in us so that the world will believe you sent me. . . . May they experience such perfect unity that the world will know that you sent me and that you love them as much as you love me."

Jesus, please help us be a unified team so that we can win at sharing Your love and truth. Amen.

Look at Jesus, Not at the Storms

*Peter got out of the boat and walked
on the water and came to Jesus.*
MATTHEW 14:28–29 ESV

Once when Jesus went off to pray alone, the disciples were in a boat traveling on ahead of Him. In the middle of the night, He walked out on the lake to catch up with them. The disciples were terrified. But Jesus said to them, "It's me! Don't be afraid." As soon as the disciple Peter realized it was Jesus out on the lake, he wanted to walk on water too. And he trusted that Jesus could enable him. So he climbed out of the boat and started walking on the waves toward Jesus. But then something changed, and he began to sink. Peter had taken his focus off Jesus and put it on the wind and waves instead. The same thing will happen to us if we're not careful. We must keep looking to Jesus through every storm in life. If we do, He'll keep us steady. If we don't, we'll sink.

---

*Jesus, I want to look at You, not at the storms
in life. Please help me to keep choosing You and
depending on Your awesome power! Amen.*

There's Only One to Worship

"Worship the Lord your God, and serve him only."
MATTHEW 4:10 NIV

Flee from the worship of idols.
1 CORINTHIANS 10:14 NLT

When you hear the word *idol*, do you think of some big stone statue in ancient times? It may seem ridiculous to those of us who love Jesus to think it possible to have an idol. Why would anyone worship some object made of metal or stone that just sits there? But did you know that idols can actually be anything we put above Jesus on our list of priorities? Jesus wants us to focus on Him first and then let all the other good things in our lives—like our family and friends, our church and activities, our schoolwork and jobs, our fun possessions like our phones, music, clothes, jewelry, etc.—fall into place in good order below Him on the list. When He is first, He helps us succeed in the best ways possible with everything else.

Jesus, I'm grateful for all the good things in my life, but I don't want to worship them. I worship You alone. Please help me to stick to this promise. Amen.

Jesus Warns about Anger

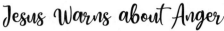

"You have heard that our ancestors were told, 'You must not murder. If you commit murder, you are subject to judgment.' But I say, if you are even angry with someone, you are subject to judgment! If you call someone an idiot, you are in danger of being brought before the court. And if you curse someone, you are in danger of the fires of hell."
MATTHEW 5:21–22 NLT

Jesus taught some very serious warnings about anger, so it's obviously important that we don't let angry emotions overwhelm us and make us feel out of control. We should constantly ask Jesus to help us deal with anger wisely and well. Look up more scriptures like these for help too:

- "A kind answer soothes angry feelings, but harsh words stir them up" (Proverbs 15:1 CEV).

- "'Don't sin by letting anger control you.' Don't let the sun go down while you are still angry, for anger gives a foothold to the devil" (Ephesians 4:26–27 NLT).

Jesus, my anger can get out of hand so easily. Please help me to remember Your warnings and control it. Amen.

What We Were Before

Once we, too, were foolish and disobedient. We were misled and became slaves to many lusts and pleasures. Our lives were full of evil and envy, and we hated each other. But when God our Savior revealed his kindness and love, he saved us, not because of the righteous things we had done, but because of his mercy. He washed away our sins, giving us a new birth and new life through the Holy Spirit.
TITUS 3:3–5 NLT

Don't try to keep past mistakes secret from Jesus. You couldn't if you tried, because He sees all and knows all anyway. The Bible says, "While we were still sinners, Christ died for us" (Romans 5:8 NIV). He didn't die for perfect people without sin. Those people don't even exist except for Jesus! He alone can offer us grace and salvation from sin because He suffered and died on the cross to pay the price for sin.

Jesus, You know my past, and yet You saved me, You love me, and You give me new life. I'm so very grateful. Amen.

Choose Jesus above All Other Friends

Don't fool yourselves. Bad friends will destroy you. Be sensible and stop sinning.
1 CORINTHIANS 15:33–34 CEV

Friendships are fun, and we need them in our lives! But we need to be very careful about them. Our very best friend should always be Jesus, the Savior we live for. The next best friends should be those who love and follow Him and try to be as much like Him as possible. A bad friend will lead you into trouble and away from Jesus. We need God's help in choosing and keeping friends, so we should never stop asking God to show us every friend's true character—and which friendships to enjoy and which ones to walk away from.

Jesus, thank You for the gift of good friends. Please guide me in friendship and help me to be careful who my friends are. Help me to be brave enough to walk away from friendships that are bad for me. Amen.

Amazing Joy and Peace

Always be full of joy in the Lord. I say it again—rejoice!... Don't worry about anything; instead, pray about everything. Tell God what you need, and thank him for all he has done. Then you will experience God's peace, which exceeds anything we can understand. His peace will guard your hearts and minds as you live in Christ Jesus.
PHILIPPIANS 4:4, 6–7 NLT

No matter what hard or sad thing you might have going on, you have reason to be full of joy because you have chosen Jesus as your Savior. You can give all your worries to Jesus because He cares for you (1 Peter 5:7). And as you trust in Him and pray to Him for your needs, thanking Him for who He is and all He does, you will have inexplicable peace and joy that are so out-of-this-world amazing!

Jesus, I'm so thankful that You replace my worries and troubles with amazing joy and peace! Amen.

Follow Your Good Shepherd

[Jesus said:] "My sheep hear my voice, and I know them, and they follow me. I give them eternal life, and they will never perish, and no one will snatch them out of my hand. My Father, who has given them to me, is greater than all, and no one is able to snatch them out of the Father's hand. I and the Father are one."
JOHN 10:27–30 ESV

Jesus is your Good Shepherd, and you are one of His sheep. He cares for you, protects you, and provides for you. You don't need to be worried about any hard situations or scared of any earthly dangers, because God holds you in His hand in this life. And your true home is in heaven, where you will live forever in perfect joy and peace.

Jesus, You are my Good Shepherd. Thank You for loving me, guiding me, protecting me, and providing for me. Thank You for life, joy, love, and peace that last forever. Amen.

Love for the Truth

*The Lord hates lying lips, but those
who speak the truth are His joy.*
PROVERBS 12:22 NLV

We must stand strong and depend on Jesus for real truth, especially since the world seems to get more and more confused about what the truth is. And since He hates lying lips, so should we! That means we should tell the truth about everything—big things and little things. In Luke 16:10 (NLT), Jesus says, "If you are faithful in little things, you will be faithful in large ones. But if you are dishonest in little things, you won't be honest with greater responsibilities." When we tell the truth, people can trust us and Jesus will bless us. He will be full of joy because of us.

---

*Jesus, please help me to love the truth and never to
lie, even about little things. If I mess up, help me to
confess and make things right with Your wisdom.
I want to be trustworthy in all things. Amen.*

Like Fruit Trees

[Jesus said:] "Just as you can identify a tree by its fruit, so you can identify people by their actions."
MATTHEW 7:20 NLT

When someone chooses Jesus as Savior and has a true relationship with Him, they are a bit like a good fruit tree. Just like a fruit tree is only healthy and growing well if it produces fruit, Christians are only healthy and growing well if they produce good fruit—meaning the good deeds they do in their lives, the way they care for others, and the actions and habits that clearly show they love and follow Jesus and live by His Word. The good things we do are not what gain us salvation, but we were created to do good things. As we trust and follow Jesus, He brings us opportunities to do those good things (Ephesians 2:10).

Jesus, please help me produce all the good fruit You want me to. Keep me growing strong in my relationship with You! Amen.

Just Cry Sometimes

Jesus started crying.
JOHN 11:35 CEV

Jesus cried, and so should we sometimes. Maybe because of frustration and sadness. Maybe we just need time and space to feel our emotions and pray about them. If we try to ignore emotions and bottle them up, they often explode in other ways or make us feel sick inside. So we don't ever need to feel that crying means we're weak. Listening to and figuring out where our emotions are coming from and giving them time and space to release actually take a lot of maturity and strength. When we can identify emotions and realize the source of them, they don't have to overwhelm us or make us act out in unhealthy ways. Telling Jesus and others we trust all about our emotions is one of the very best ways to deal with them.

Jesus, give me wisdom about letting myself cry sometimes like You did. Help me listen to my emotions and figure out how to handle them in healthy ways. Amen.

Choose Jesus and Never Be Alone

Where can I go from Your Spirit? Or where can I run away from where You are? If I go up to heaven, You are there! If I make my bed in the place of the dead, You are there! If I take the wings of the morning or live in the farthest part of the sea, even there Your hand will lead me and Your right hand will hold me.
PSALM 139:7–10 NLV

There is no place on earth where you are ever away from Jesus. Through His Spirit, He is with you every single second of every single day, no matter where you go and what you do. He sees and knows everything, even everything you think! That should never bother you; it should make you feel loved and cared for. Jesus wants to help, guide, and protect you anytime and anywhere.

Jesus, thank You for being my constant companion. You are always there, everywhere! I'm never alone and have nothing to fear when I depend on You! Amen.

Ask Jesus Hard Questions

*Has the Lord rejected me forever? Will he never again be kind to me? Is his unfailing love gone forever? Have his promises permanently failed? Has God forgotten to be gracious? Has he slammed the door on his compassion?... But then I recall all you have done, O L*ORD*; I remember your wonderful deeds of long ago. They are constantly in my thoughts. I cannot stop thinking about your mighty works.*
PSALM 77:7–9, 11–12 NLT

Jesus can handle all your hard questions. It's okay to ask Him about them. Maybe you're struggling with rejection, sadness, pain, or all of those right now, just like the writer of this psalm was. Sometimes in the midst of something awful, we wonder where Jesus is and if He's forgotten to take care of us. So we need to focus hard on remembering all the good things He has done for us in the past, in His perfect timing, and trust that He will continue.

Jesus, I just need to know You are near while I ask You these hard questions. Please draw me close, and help me remember all of Your truth and goodness and love. Amen.

When People Mock You

[Jesus said:] "God blesses you when people mock you and persecute you and lie about you and say all sorts of evil things against you because you are my followers. Be happy about it! Be very glad! For a great reward awaits you in heaven."
MATTHEW 5:11–12 NLT

It's really hard to think being made fun of is a blessing, but Jesus tells us to celebrate it! God hears each instance, He's keeping track, and He rewards loyalty and love for Him. If you're ever made fun of because you follow Jesus, remember this scripture. Jesus knows every moment that you ever suffer for Him, and He will make everything right one day.

Jesus, help me to keep the right perspective if I'm made fun of for following You. I trust that You know and care about it and that You will protect and bless me. Amen.

Jesus Is Your Confidence

The Lord will be your confidence.
PROVERBS 3:26 ESV

After we do something embarrassing or awkward—and who hasn't?—the weird, awful feelings can live on in our minds endlessly. But it's usually a much bigger deal in our own minds than in the minds of others. Yes, whoever was watching might remember for a while. You might even get teased. But that shows others' bad character, not yours. You can choose to show strong, good character by remembering that everyone has embarrassing moments and just shaking it off. Hold your head high and look to Jesus, remembering that you belong to Him and He is your confidence.

Jesus, when I'm dealing with embarrassment, please help me to shake it off. Remind me that I am Yours and You are my confidence. Thank You for loving me no matter what. Amen.

Bring Him Your Heavy Loads

[Jesus said:] "Come to Me, all of you who work and have heavy loads. I will give you rest. Follow My teachings and learn from Me. I am gentle and do not have pride. You will have rest for your souls. For My way of carrying a load is easy and My load is not heavy."
MATTHEW 11:28–30 NLV

What heavy stuff are you carrying today? Maybe it's a big school project that needs lots of work, or maybe there is lots of drama among your friends. Maybe you're fighting with someone in your family. Whatever it is, take it to Jesus and He will help you with it. He will help you feel peaceful and rested. Ask Him what to do about your heavy load, and then listen and let Him teach you through prayer and His Word.

Jesus, I need You to help with this hard and heavy load. I need Your rest and peace. Please guide me and show me how to deal with the difficult things going on in my life the way You want me to. Amen.

Choose Compassion and Care

Jesus said: "A man was going down from Jerusalem to Jericho, when he was attacked by robbers. They stripped him of his clothes, beat him and went away, leaving him half dead.... A Samaritan, as he traveled, came where the man was; and when he saw him, he took pity on him. He went to him and bandaged his wounds, pouring on oil and wine. Then he put the man on his own donkey, brought him to an inn and took care of him."
LUKE 10:30, 33–34 NIV

Jesus shared a story about how two people just walked by and ignored a poor man who had been robbed and beaten and left for dead. But then a Samaritan man came along and helped the stranger, going above and beyond to make sure he was well cared for. Jesus wants us to choose compassion and care for others, just like the Samaritan man did.

Jesus, like You taught, I want to choose compassion for those who are in need. Show me the ways You want me to care for others. Amen.

No Worries with Jesus

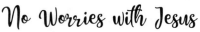

[Jesus said:] "Look at the birds. They don't plant or harvest or store food in barns, for your heavenly Father feeds them. And aren't you far more valuable to him than they are? Can all your worries add a single moment to your life? And why worry about your clothing? Look at the lilies of the field and how they grow. . . . If God cares so wonderfully for wildflowers that are here today and thrown into the fire tomorrow, he will certainly care for you. Why do you have so little faith? So don't worry about these things. . . . Your heavenly Father already knows all your needs. Seek the Kingdom of God above all else, and live righteously, and he will give you everything you need."
MATTHEW 6:26–28, 30–33 NLT

Jesus taught clearly that we aren't supposed to worry, because our heavenly Father knows exactly what we need and will provide it. If He knows and takes good care of even the birds and the flowers that He created, He definitely will take even better care of the people He made in His own image.

Jesus, thank You for teaching me why I don't need to worry. Amen.

Awesome Joy!

Though you have not seen [Jesus Christ], you love him; and even though you do not see him now, you believe in him and are filled with an inexpressible and glorious joy, for you are receiving the end result of your faith, the salvation of your souls.
1 PETER 1:8–9 NIV

Happy feelings come and go in this life. But for those who choose Jesus as Savior, real joy—inexpressible and glorious joy!—comes from knowing, loving, and trusting Him. We know that we are saved from our sin, and that confidence is incredible! We can return to God's Word to let scripture stir up real joy inside us every single day.

Jesus, I praise and thank You so much for the inexpressible and glorious joy You fill me with inside because I know I am loved and saved by You! Amen.

Be Honest and Faithful, Even with the Little Things

"You are a good and faithful servant. I left you in charge of only a little, but now I will put you in charge of much more. Come and share in my happiness!"
MATTHEW 25:21 CEV

Have you ever been in a situation where you were leaving the store and realized you accidentally didn't pay for an item, but no one noticed? It's happened to nearly everyone, and we all have a choice in that moment to keep the item or be honest about it and let a cashier know we still need to pay for something. We need to remember Jesus' teaching that when we are faithful and honest with even the little things, He can trust us to be faithful and honest with bigger blessings and responsibilities.

Jesus, You see all my actions, both big and small. I believe You bless me when You see I'm trustworthy. Please help me to be a person of honesty and integrity in all things, and if I make mistakes, I'm grateful for Your grace. Please help me make them right. Amen.

Stay Joined to Jesus

I am the true vine, and my Father is the gardener.
JOHN 15:1 CEV

Jesus used an example of a grapevine to show us how we can produce fruit—meaning how we can do good things in our lives for God's glory—and to help us understand how God answers our prayers:

> "Stay joined to me, and I will stay joined to you. Just as a branch cannot produce fruit unless it stays joined to the vine, you cannot produce fruit unless you stay joined to me. I am the vine, and you are the branches. If you stay joined to me, and I stay joined to you, then you will produce lots of fruit. But you cannot do anything without me. If you don't stay joined to me, you will be thrown away. You will be like dry branches that are gathered up and burned in a fire. Stay joined to me and let my teachings become part of you. Then you can pray for whatever you want, and your prayer will be answered." JOHN 15:4–7 CEV

---

*Jesus, I want to stay joined to You.
It's the very best place to be. Amen.*

His Love Is Unstoppable

Who shall separate us from the love of Christ? Shall trouble or hardship or persecution or famine or nakedness or danger or sword?... No, in all these things we are more than conquerors through him who loved us. For I am convinced that neither death nor life, neither angels nor demons, neither the present nor the future, nor any powers, neither height nor depth, nor anything else in all creation, will be able to separate us from the love of God that is in Christ Jesus our Lord.
ROMANS 8:35, 37–39 NIV

Everyone who chooses Jesus as Savior chooses unstoppable love. The Bible promises that even the strongest forces, the most extreme circumstances, and the very worst things of this world can't keep away God's amazing love for us through Jesus.

Jesus, thank You that absolutely nothing can stop Your awesome love for me or keep me away from it. Amen.

Light in the Darkness

Again Jesus spoke to them, saying, "I am the light of the world. Whoever follows me will not walk in darkness, but will have the light of life."
JOHN 8:12 ESV

Do you ever take time to just enjoy the beautiful night sky and praise God for His amazing creation of stars and galaxies and all the heavens? Of course, it has to be dark outside in order to see the stars—the darker the better, actually. That's a good fact to think about if we're ever feeling discouraged about how dark our world seems to be getting with sin growing so popular and being flaunted all around us. We have to remember that light shines brighter in darkness. When we've chosen Jesus as Savior and we have the Holy Spirit within us, we are shining His light in a very dark world. And when we learn and live by and share God's Word, we spread His light too, for the Bible is a lamp for our feet and a light to all our paths (Psalm 119:105).

Jesus, please help me to shine brightly in a dark world, pointing others to You so they will choose You as Savior. Amen.

Be Willing to Share

A rich man's farm produced a big crop.... Later, he said, "Now I know what I'll do. I'll tear down my barns and build bigger ones, where I can store all my grain and other goods. Then I'll say to myself, 'You have stored up enough good things to last for years to come. Live it up! Eat, drink, and enjoy yourself.'" But God said to him, "You fool! Tonight you will die. Then who will get what you have stored up?" "This is what happens to people who store up everything for themselves, but are poor in the sight of God."
LUKE 12:16, 18–21 CEV

In this parable, Jesus taught that when we have a lot, we should be willing to share it with others. No person has any idea exactly how long they will live on this earth. It's far better to be generous to others than to store it all selfishly. Our goal should be to have the riches of God, not the riches of this world.

Jesus, help me to be generous with my money and possessions. Please give me a desire and joy for sharing with others. Amen.

Let "Weak" Mean "Strong"

[Jesus said:] "My grace is sufficient for you, for my power is made perfect in weakness." Therefore I will boast all the more gladly about my weaknesses, so that Christ's power may rest on me. That is why, for Christ's sake, I delight in weaknesses, in insults, in hardships, in persecutions, in difficulties. For when I am weak, then I am strong.
2 CORINTHIANS 12:9–10 NIV

Jesus does not want us to be strong on our own. That's not because He's mean and selfish. It's because He wants us to be truly strong, the best kind of strong—strong because we are dependent on Him and full of His power, not our own.

Jesus, help me to be happy to be weak on my own because that means I must get real strength from You. I'm only truly strong when I'm choosing to depend on You for everything. Thank You for wanting the very best for me and filling me with Your power and love. Amen.

Be on Guard

Jesus said to them all, "Watch yourselves! Keep from wanting all kinds of things you should not have. A man's life is not made up of things, even if he has many riches."
LUKE 12:15 NLV

A huge problem with social media these days is that it creates jealousy in us. We all struggle with feelings of jealousy anyway, even if we spend zero time on social media. So constantly staring at cool pictures and posts about what everyone else has and the experiences and relationships they're enjoying has huge potential to create even more feelings of envy in us. And Jesus strongly warned us about envy, jealousy, and greed. We have to be on guard to keep our thoughts and desires fixed on what Jesus wants for us and to be content with the blessings He's already given.

Jesus, it's so easy to look at the lives of others and want what they have rather than to simply be content with my own life and blessings. Please help me to be on guard against comparison and jealousy and greed. I want to remember Your good warnings. Amen.

Because of Jesus, God Forgives

*If you, Lord, should write down our sins,
O Lord, who could stand? But You are the One
Who forgives, so You are honored with fear.
I wait for the Lord. My soul waits and I hope
in His Word. . . . For there is loving-kindness
with the Lord. With Him we are saved for sure.
And He will save Israel from all their sins.*
PSALM 130:3–5, 7–8 NLV

Have you ever felt like you've messed up so badly and made such a big mistake or so many mistakes that you can never be okay again? Most everyone can relate. But because of Jesus, God is the one who forgives. We can come to Him, no matter how badly we've messed up. We can admit our sin and let Him cover us with His mercy and grace.

Jesus, I can't believe I messed up this much. I'm so sorry. I admit what I did, and I need Your help to turn away from this sin and get back on track following You. I need Your grace and mercy so much, and I'm so very grateful for how lovingly You give it. Amen.

Incredible Power

I pray that the great God and Father of our Lord Jesus Christ may give you the wisdom of His Spirit. Then you will be able to understand the secrets about Him as you know Him better. . . . I pray that you will see how great the things are that He has promised to those who belong to Him. I pray that you will know how great His power is for those who have put their trust in Him. It is the same power that raised Christ from the dead.
EPHESIANS 1:17–20 NLV

These prayers that Paul wrote in Ephesians are still what Jesus wants for you as a Christian today. If you have chosen Jesus as Savior, you belong to Him and have hope for the awesome things He has planned for you. And His power for you is so great—it is the same power that brought Him back to life! That incredible power is working in you now as you serve Jesus and live for Him, and it will be working in you forever because it has given you eternal life.

Jesus, help me to see and know more and more every day how awesome You are and how awesome Your plans and Your power in my life are. Amen.

Though Sins Are Like Scarlet

"Come now, let us settle the matter," says the LORD. "Though your sins are like scarlet, they shall be as white as snow; though they are red as crimson, they shall be like wool."

ISAIAH 1:18 NIV

Don't ever forget that Jesus can clean up the darkest stains of sin. Because of His grace, He removes us from our sin and mistakes and helps us get back on track. He helps us work them out for good and His glory so that we can share our stories with others and help them see His grace too. Praise Him for that! He's the only one who can take the ugliest, filthiest things away and make us as clean as freshly fallen snow!

Jesus, I praise You for Your power over sin! I confess these sins to You: _____. I'm so sorry, and I need Your grace to cover them and Your help to overcome them. Amen.

Forever Treasure

[Jesus said:] Don't store up treasures on earth! Moths and rust can destroy them, and thieves can break in and steal them. Instead, store up your treasures in heaven, where moths and rust cannot destroy them, and thieves cannot break in and steal them. Your heart will always be where your treasure is.
MATTHEW 6:19–21 CEV

All the cool things we have in this world are nice, for sure, like clothes and jewelry and makeup and decor and the fun things we collect. And it's okay to enjoy those things—as long as we don't worship them, making it our main goal and motivation to get more stuff. Nothing on this earth lasts forever. Things break or get old or end up lost. Entertainment and vacations come to an end. You can't take one bit of your stuff to heaven when your life on earth is over. So Jesus taught us to store up treasures in heaven. That's where our blessings last forever. How do we store treasure in heaven? We ask God to show us the good works He has planned for us to do, and we love, follow, and obey Him.

Jesus, help me focus more on what You taught about treasure in heaven. Amen.

Sincerely, Not Showy

[Jesus said:] "When you pray, do not be as those who pretend to be someone they are not. They love to stand and pray in the places of worship or in the streets so people can see them.... When you pray, go into a room by yourself. After you have shut the door, pray to your Father Who is in secret. Then your Father Who sees in secret will reward you."
MATTHEW 6:5–6 NLV

Jesus taught us to pray sincerely, directly to our heavenly Father—and not for attention or to make ourselves look good. Our prayers should be real conversation—praising Him, asking for His help, and learning from Him.

Does this scripture passage mean that every prayer should be said in secret, when we're alone? No. But in every prayer, we should want all attention on God and His power alone, not on ourselves.

Jesus, help me to put all attention on You in prayer and praise. Amen.

He Won't Change

*Jesus Christ is the same yesterday
and today and forever.*
HEBREWS 13:8 NLV

Nothing about life will always stay the same, and sometimes we just wish it would! That's why we can be so thankful that God gave us Jesus, who is always dependable and always the same—yesterday, today, and forever! Psalm 102:25–27 (NLV) says, "You made the earth in the beginning. You made the heavens with Your hands. They will be destroyed but You will always live. They will all become old as clothing becomes old. You will change them like a coat. And they will be changed, but You are always the same. Your years will never end."

Jesus is *never* going to let you down, so lean on Him and ask Him to hold you steady when life seems crazy. Talk to Him about all of your joys, all of your fears, and all of your needs.

---

*Jesus, thank You for always being my dependable
Savior through all of life's ups and downs! Amen.*

Serve Your Savior

Then the ones who pleased the Lord will ask, "When did we give you something to eat or drink? When did we welcome you as a stranger or give you clothes to wear or visit you while you were sick or in jail?" The king will answer, "Whenever you did it for any of my people, no matter how unimportant they seemed, you did it for me."
MATTHEW 25:37–40 CEV

Jesus taught that whenever those who love Him help someone in need, it's like we're helping Jesus Himself. So who in your life is needy right now? What can you do and give to help and encourage those people? If you can't think of anyone, ask Jesus to show you who He wants you to help and the best ways to do so.

Jesus, thank You that I can serve You and show my love to You by serving others who are in need. Amen.

When Someone Sins against You

"If another believer sins against you, go privately and point out the offense. If the other person listens and confesses it, you have won that person back."
MATTHEW 18:15 NLT

Jesus taught how to deal with conflict with fellow believers in the right ways. If someone has sinned against us, hurt us, or upset us, we may need to have hard conversations to work things out and improve the relationship and situation. It can be so hard, but it's not right to talk about the offending person behind his or her back. Jesus taught us to go to that person privately first. We should pray for Jesus to give us peace and wisdom and to help us embrace good communication and good conflict. We can choose to obey Jesus when we've been mistreated.

Jesus, please help me to choose to obey You when someone sins against me. I want to handle it the right way—Your way. Amen.

Choose Jesus, Even under Peer Pressure

Do not want to be like those who do wrong.... Trust in the Lord, and do good. So you will live in the land and will be fed. Be happy in the Lord. And He will give you the desires of your heart.
PSALM 37:1, 3–4 NLV

It seems like those who do wrong are everywhere we turn. And sometimes it seems like no big deal to be like them and just go along with whatever seems popular, even if we know deep down that what is popular is wrong. It takes mental strength and courage to not join those doing wrong, especially if we're feeling pressure from people we thought were good friends. But God promises that if we trust Him and do good, we will have everything we need, and He will give us the things that make us truly happy—because first we're happy in Him!

Jesus, please help me to stand strong and choose to obey You even under peer pressure. I want to do what makes You happy. I trust that's the best way for me to be truly happy too. Amen.

Life Again

We want you to know for sure about those who have died. You have no reason to have sorrow as those who have no hope. We believe that Jesus died and then came to life again. Because we believe this, we know that God will bring to life again all those who belong to Jesus.
1 THESSALONIANS 4:13–14 NLV

When someone we love dies, it's sad and painful, and we miss them like crazy. And it's so hard not to be able to share our lives with them or hug them or call them. But for all who choose Jesus as Savior, this life on earth is only the beginning. We have new life and perfect heaven to look forward to, where we will spend forever with Jesus along with all our loved ones who chose Him too. If you have loved ones who have not yet chosen to trust in Jesus, keep praying for them.

Thank You, Jesus, that I don't have to grieve without hope. Thank You for peace and comfort in knowing that I will see my loved ones who have died but chose You as Savior. Amen.

Salt of the Earth and Light of the World

"You are the salt of the earth. But what good is salt if it has lost its flavor?... You are the light of the world—like a city on a hilltop that cannot be hidden.... In the same way, let your good deeds shine out for all to see, so that everyone will praise your heavenly Father."
MATTHEW 5:13–14, 16 NLT

Jesus taught that we should want to be like salt and light. Salt helps food taste its best, and we should want to bring out the best in others and help show them life at its very best. Life at its best is a life that believes in and follows Jesus. Jesus also wants us to be the light of the world. If we hide our light, we can't help others see the way to Jesus. But if we shine our light, giving Him honor through every good thing we do, we help others honor Him too.

Jesus, I want to reach out to others and be salt and light to them, helping them know and love You too! Amen.

Angels: Fact or Fiction?

[Jesus said:] "Be sure you do not hate one of these little children. I tell you, they have angels who are always looking into the face of My Father in heaven."
MATTHEW 18:10 NLV

While stories and movies might give us some false ideas about what angels do and what they look like, they are real. Jesus said so! So don't forget about angels. Study the Bible to truly learn about them. Ask Jesus to send His help, care, and protection through them. Let these scriptures teach and encourage you:

- "The angel of the Lord stays close around those who fear Him, and He takes them out of trouble" (Psalm 34:7 NLV).

- "Keep on loving each other as Christian brothers. Do not forget to be kind to strangers and let them stay in your home. Some people have had angels in their homes without knowing it" (Hebrews 13:1–2 NLV).

Jesus, it's so comforting and gives me such confidence to know that I am so loved and protected, even by supernatural angels— all because I have chosen You! Amen.

Be Proud of the Lord

If anyone wants to be proud, he should be proud of what the Lord has done.
2 CORINTHIANS 10:17 NLV

How do you like to celebrate when you reach a goal or accomplish something you've been working hard at? Of course you should feel happy and excited, but we all have to be careful that we don't forget to give our Lord Jesus credit when we're celebrating. It's a great way to stay humble and never become full of pride in ourselves. Our Lord deserves all the best praise and worship because He created us and gave us our gifts, talents, and abilities.

Lord Jesus, You are the one who gives me everything and makes me capable of accomplishing great things. Please help me to use my gifts well in the ways You want me to, and help me to point others to choosing You as Savior. Amen.

Call on Jesus to Stop the Storm

A bad wind storm came up. The waves were coming over the side of the boat. It was filling up with water. Jesus was in the back part of the boat sleeping on a pillow. [The disciples] woke Him up, crying out, "Teacher, do You not care that we are about to die?" He got up and spoke sharp words to the wind. He said to the sea, "Be quiet! Be still." At once the wind stopped blowing. There were no more waves. He said to His followers, "Why are you so full of fear? Do you not have faith?"
MARK 4:37–40 NLV

Jesus' disciples were absolutely terrified during the storm described in Mark 4. Yet it took only a few words from Jesus to make everything okay. Through the Holy Spirit, that same powerful, storm-stopping presence of Jesus is with you this moment! No matter what is scaring you right now, call on Jesus and ask Him to make a way through the storm for you.

Jesus, You are capable of simply speaking the words and calming anything down. I call on You now for Your help with the storm I'm facing in my life. Amen.

Jesus Has Compassion

A man with leprosy came and knelt in front of Jesus, begging to be healed. "If you are willing, you can heal me and make me clean," he said. Moved with compassion, Jesus reached out and touched him. "I am willing," he said. "Be healed!" Instantly the leprosy disappeared, and the man was healed.... The man went and spread the word, proclaiming to everyone what had happened. As a result, large crowds soon surrounded Jesus, and he couldn't publicly enter a town anywhere. He had to stay out in the secluded places, but people from everywhere kept coming to him.
MARK 1:40–42, 45 NLT

Most people in Bible times would never touch or go near a person with leprosy, but Jesus was "moved with compassion" and reached out and touched the man who begged him to make him clean from his skin disease. Instantly, the man was healed. How relieved and happy he must have felt! He wanted to share with everyone who would listen about what Jesus had done for Him.

Jesus, Your power to heal is amazing! Thank You for Your compassion. Help me to share with others what You are doing in my life too. Amen.

Keep a Clear Mind

For a time is coming when people will no longer listen to sound and wholesome teaching. They will follow their own desires and will look for teachers who will tell them whatever their itching ears want to hear. They will reject the truth and chase after myths. But you should keep a clear mind in every situation.
2 TIMOTHY 4:3–5 NLT

There's a lot of good stuff out there in movies, shows, books, music, magazines, and endless websites and social media. But there's a lot of really awful stuff too. We make it harder and harder to listen to Jesus if we fill our minds with too much media. That's why, in such a confusing world with so many false teachers, it's more important than ever to be extra, *extra* careful what we watch, read, and listen to (and how much) and what activities we participate in. Jesus is always so near through His Holy Spirit, but how much do we tune Him out by the junk we keep jamming into our brains?

Jesus, help me empty my mind of the things that aren't good for me. I want to keep my mind clear so that I can easily hear the best things from You. Amen.

Choose Joy Each Day

*This is the day that the Lord has made.
Let us be full of joy and be glad in it.*
PSALM 118:24 NLV

Some days feel like there is absolutely nothing good in them. Big and little things go wrong, and we feel discouraged and defeated. Although things may feel awful, God's Word doesn't change based on our feelings. His Word says, "This is the day that the Lord has made. Let us be full of joy and be glad in it." We can find reasons for joy in the midst of any bad day—and the best reason for joy is that nothing can separate us from God's love or take away the eternal life that He gives us when we choose to trust in Jesus Christ alone as Savior.

---

*Jesus, I want to be full of joy in each new day,
no matter what is going on. Remind me every moment
that real joy comes from choosing You! Amen.*

His Heart Overflowed with Compassion

A funeral procession was coming out as [Jesus] approached the village gate. The young man who had died was a widow's only son, and a large crowd from the village was with her. When the Lord saw her, his heart overflowed with compassion. "Don't cry!" he said. Then he walked over to the coffin and touched it, and the bearers stopped. "Young man," he said, "I tell you, get up." Then the dead boy sat up and began to talk! And Jesus gave him back to his mother.
LUKE 7:12–15 NLT

In Bible times, if a woman had no husband and no sons, she was in a dangerous situation. It was very hard for a woman to provide for herself and protect herself without a man back then. So when Jesus saw this widow whose only son had just died, "his heart overflowed with compassion." Then Jesus brought her dead son back to life and gave him back to his mother. Can you imagine how happy she must have been?

Jesus, thank You for Your miracles! You care so much about people who are in sad situations. Help me to care like You do. Amen.

Build Others Up in Jesus

We should help others do what is right and build them up in the Lord. For even Christ didn't live to please himself.
ROMANS 15:2–3 NLT

All of us who have chosen Jesus as Savior need to intentionally encourage each other, and sometimes just the smallest ways mean so much. With simply a cheerful attitude and smile, we can spread joy. With a phone call or text, we can build someone else up. We can share hugs, scriptures, and prayer for others in need or who simply could use an extra bright spot in their day. We can remember to "let everything you say be good and helpful, so that your words will be an encouragement to those who hear them" (Ephesians 4:29 NLT).

Jesus, please remind me every day how easy it is to encourage others, lift their spirits, and build them in our faith in You. Show me who to encourage today. Amen.

Confess to Jesus

If we say we have no sin, we deceive ourselves, and the truth is not in us. If we confess our sins, he is faithful and just to forgive us our sins and to cleanse us from all unrighteousness.
1 JOHN 1:8–9 ESV

We sometimes avoid certain people because we don't want to admit how our mistakes affected them or hurt them. We do that to Jesus sometimes too. We avoid Him because we don't want to admit the ways we are disobeying Him. But He's so full of love and forgiveness for us. He wants us to simply admit our bad choices, turn away from them, and then turn back to Him. He wants us to follow Him because He wants us to have the very best kind of life and rewards, both now and forever.

Jesus, I admit my sins, and I need Your help to turn away from them. Thank You for Your generous love, grace, and forgiveness. Amen.

Jesus Prayed, "Not What I Want"

Jesus came with them to a place called Gethsemane. He said to them, "You sit here while I go over there to pray." He took Peter and the two sons of Zebedee with Him. He began to have much sorrow and a heavy heart. Then He said to them, "My soul is very sad. My soul is so full of sorrow I am ready to die. You stay here and watch with Me." He went on a little farther and got down with His face on the ground. He prayed, "My Father, if it can be done, take away what is before Me. Even so, not what I want but what You want."
MATTHEW 26:36–39 NLV

Even though Jesus was all-knowing God in human form, He had extreme sorrow and a heavy heart as He thought about what He was to endure on the cross. He honestly pleaded for God to find another way than His death on the cross. But ultimately, He prayed not for His will to be done but for God's will to be done.

Jesus, thank You for enduring the cross to pay for my sins. And thank You for Your example of obedience. I also want to pray for not my will but Yours. Amen.

To Truly Follow Jesus

Then Jesus said to his disciples, "Whoever wants to be my disciple must deny themselves and take up their cross and follow me. For whoever wants to save their life will lose it, but whoever loses their life for me will find it. What good will it be for someone to gain the whole world, yet forfeit their soul? Or what can anyone give in exchange for their soul? For the Son of Man is going to come in his Father's glory with his angels, and then he will reward each person according to what they have done."
MATTHEW 16:24–27 NIV

Jesus' message in this scripture is quite a contrast to the popular messages of today, like "Follow your own heart," "Live your truth," "Practice self-care," and "Do whatever makes you happy." Truly following Jesus means giving up any plans we have for our life and saying, "Your will be done with my life, Jesus." The best, most rewarding, most fulfilling kind of life comes from being totally committed to Him.

Jesus, help me realize more and more each day how good it is to truly live for You. Amen.

Give and Help with a Humble Heart

"Watch out! Don't do your good deeds publicly, to be admired by others, for you will lose the reward from your Father in heaven. When you give to someone in need, don't do as the hypocrites do— blowing trumpets in the synagogues and streets to call attention to their acts of charity! I tell you the truth, they have received all the reward they will ever get. But when you give to someone in need, don't let your left hand know what your right hand is doing. Give your gifts in private, and your Father, who sees everything, will reward you."

MATTHEW 6:1–4 NLT

It feels so good to help and care for others, but Jesus taught us not to be show-offs about it. Some people only give and help others to gain attention for themselves, and that's not right. When we're humble and give and help with an attitude of serving Jesus for the joy of it, we will be blessed with the forever kind of blessings.

Jesus, help me to always give and help others with the right motives and attitude like You taught. Amen.

Choose Life to the Full

[Jesus said:] "I am the gate; whoever enters through me will be saved. They will come in and go out, and find pasture. The thief comes only to steal and kill and destroy; I have come that they may have life, and have it to the full."
JOHN 10:9–10 NIV

Our enemy, the devil, is a thief, a killer, and a destroyer. But no matter what he tries to do to us, he cannot win. We will ultimately win against him in the end because of Jesus. The devil might hurt us or make us stumble away from Jesus at times, but he will never totally defeat us if Jesus is our Savior. When we choose Jesus as Savior, He gives us life to the full, and no one can ever take that away.

Jesus, thank You so much that nothing can ever take away my most valuable gift of eternal life. I choose You as my Savior. Amen.

Jesus' Power over Demons

When Jesus stepped ashore, he was met by a demon-possessed man from the town. For a long time this man had not worn clothes or lived in a house, but had lived in the tombs. When he saw Jesus, he cried out and fell at his feet, shouting at the top of his voice, "What do you want with me, Jesus, Son of the Most High God? I beg you, don't torture me!" For Jesus had commanded the impure spirit to come out of the man. Many times it had seized him, and though he was chained hand and foot and kept under guard, he had broken his chains and had been driven by the demon into solitary places.
LUKE 8:27–29 NIV

It can be scary to think of demons, but we can remember that Jesus has all power over them. He sent the demons out of this man and into a herd of pigs! Jesus can do anything to protect and rescue those who have faith in Him!

Jesus, when I feel afraid, remind me of Your power against any evil force. Please give me courage. Keep me close and protect me, I pray. Amen.

Be Jesus' Follower First

So don't boast about following a particular human leader. For everything belongs to you—whether Paul or Apollos or Peter, or the world, or life and death, or the present and the future. Everything belongs to you, and you belong to Christ, and Christ belongs to God.
1 CORINTHIANS 3:21–23 NLT

We all need good leaders in our lives—leaders who point us to a closer relationship with Jesus. But the Bible warns about never boasting about following any of these leaders. We should never hold them up too high, because any human can fall from their position as a good leader. Jesus alone should be the leader we follow, looking to Him and His Word for the best direction. He knows us better than anyone else and wants to lead us in the very best kind of life!

Jesus, thank You for the leaders in my life, but You are my very best leader. Please keep me close as You guide me. I never want to stop following You above all! Amen.

Let His Teaching Live in You

Let the teaching of Christ and His words keep on living in you. These make your lives rich and full of wisdom.
COLOSSIANS 3:16 NLV

If we let all of Jesus' teachings live in us—meaning we focus on, listen to, and obey them—we will have lives that are rich and full of wisdom. But *rich* in this case doesn't necessarily mean a life with lots of money; it means a life full of all the goodness God wants to give us, especially the things money can never buy. So as you make choices about what you put into your mind, ask yourself: *Does this help me focus on God and follow Jesus? If not, what can I choose instead to help me focus on Him?*

Jesus, I don't want to just read or listen to Your teaching; I want it to live in me and change my whole life. Please keep me growing closer and closer to You! Amen.

Closer, Not Farther

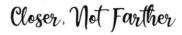

[Jesus said:] "I have told you these things, so that in me you may have peace. In this world you will have trouble. But take heart! I have overcome the world."
JOHN 16:33 NIV

In this world, all kinds of sad and terrible things can happen to us or people we know. You can probably think of a whole list of things going on right now. In any of those situations, everyone has a very important choice to make—get closer to Jesus or farther away? Choose to let Him help and comfort you, or choose to hold on to anger and blame? The wise choice is to grow closer to Jesus. Psalm 34:17–18 (NLV) says, "Those who are right with the Lord cry, and He hears them. And He takes them from all their troubles. The Lord is near to those who have a broken heart."

Jesus, please help me never to grow farther from You when my heart feels broken. Draw me closer as I remember Your love and that You want to heal my broken heart. Amen.

Just One Touch

A woman was there who had been subject to bleeding for twelve years, but no one could heal her. She came up behind [Jesus] and touched the edge of his cloak, and immediately her bleeding stopped.... Jesus said, "Someone touched me; I know that power has gone out from me." Then the woman, seeing that she could not go unnoticed, came trembling and fell at his feet. In the presence of all the people, she told why she had touched him and how she had been instantly healed. Then he said to her, "Daughter, your faith has healed you. Go in peace."
LUKE 8:43–44, 46–48 NIV

If you've ever had a cold that just never seemed to end, you know how sick of being sick you can get, even for a matter of days or weeks. The poor bleeding woman in the Bible had been sick for twelve *years*! But she had heard of Jesus, and she had great faith in His power. She was sure that if she just touched the bottom of His cloak, she would be healed. So she did, and she was!

Jesus, help me to have such awesome faith in You. Amen.

Do This in Remembrance of Jesus

[Jesus] took some bread and gave thanks to God for it. Then he broke it in pieces and gave it to the disciples, saying, "This is my body, which is given for you. Do this in remembrance of me." After supper he took another cup of wine and said, "This cup is the new covenant between God and his people—an agreement confirmed with my blood, which is poured out as a sacrifice for you."
LUKE 22:19–20 NLT

At the last supper that Jesus had with His disciples before He was crucified on the cross, He taught about what we call Communion today, which was how to think of and remember Him and His work on the cross. Nowadays, as we gather together with other believers at church, we have Communion together to eat the bread and drink the cup that represent Jesus' body and blood given in sacrifice to pay for our sins. We remember with gratitude what Jesus has done for us.

Oh Jesus, I never want to forget what You suffered to save me. Thank You for enduring all the pain and punishment of sin so that all those who choose to repent and trust in You can have eternal life. Amen.

Do Your Work for Jesus

Work for them as you would for the Lord because you honor God. Whatever work you do, do it with all your heart. Do it for the Lord and not for men. Remember that you will get your reward from the Lord. He will give you what you should receive. You are working for the Lord Christ.
COLOSSIANS 3:22–24 NLV

Sometimes your studies, work, and responsibilities can feel like too much. So take it all to Jesus. Tell Him how overwhelmed you feel. He cares about your feelings and loves to help you. You can do any task or assignment as if it's praise and honor to the Lord. Do your best at it, no matter what it is, saying: "Jesus, I want to bring glory and honor to You with the way I work at this and with my attitude in the middle of it."

Jesus, remind me that no matter what I'm working on, I can do it in a way to honor You if I focus my mind on praising and thanking You in the middle of it. Amen.

Wait for Jesus

Wait for the LORD; be strong, and let your heart take courage; wait for the LORD!
PSALM 27:14 ESV

Being patient isn't popular. We want that new thing, new opportunity, new relationship, or answer to prayer right now. But despite what the fast-paced world around us says, we can choose to think about what the Bible tells us about waiting and patience. We can learn from scriptures on this topic and look for more in His Word. We can draw close to Jesus and let Him teach us to wait well:

- "They who wait upon the Lord will get new strength. They will rise up with wings like eagles. They will run and not get tired. They will walk and not become weak" (Isaiah 40:31 NLV).

- "The Lord is good to those who wait for Him, to the one who looks for Him" (Lamentations 3:25 NLV).

- "Wait for the LORD and keep his way, and he will exalt you to inherit the land" (Psalm 37:34 ESV).

Jesus, help me to trust in Your perfect timing. Teach me the things I need to learn while I wait. Amen.

Living Water

"Sir," the woman said, "you have nothing to draw with and the well is deep. Where can you get this living water?... Jesus answered, "Everyone who drinks this water will be thirsty again, but whoever drinks the water I give them will never thirst. Indeed, the water I give them will become in them a spring of water welling up to eternal life."
JOHN 4:11, 13–14 NIV

This woman who encountered Jesus was a Samaritan woman, and normally a Jew would have nothing to do with a Samaritan. And if that wasn't shocking enough to her, Jesus then claimed to be able to give her living water—water that would become a spring welling up to eternal life. On top of that, Jesus told her how He knew everything about her. Amazed, "the woman left her water jar and ran back into town, where she said to the people, 'Come and see a man who told me everything I have ever done! Could he be the Messiah?' Everyone in town went out to see Jesus" (John 4:28–30 CEV).

Jesus, only You can offer the gift of living water welling up to eternal life. Only You know everything. Only You can save and satisfy. Amen.

Jesus on the Cross

"What shall I do, then, with the one you call the king of the Jews?" Pilate asked them. "Crucify him!" they shouted. "Why? What crime has he committed?" asked Pilate. But they shouted all the louder, "Crucify him!"
MARK 15:12–14 NIV

You can read the details of Jesus' crucifixion and death on the cross in these passages: Matthew 27, Mark 15, Luke 23, and John 19. It's important to know exactly what Jesus went through to save us. Being a Christian is not some silly choice or religion to make us feel good. It's a decision based on the work of Jesus Christ on the cross—realizing that our sins separate us from God and that there are consequences for sin. A price had to be paid for those sins to give us a way to have relationship with our Creator once again. Jesus, who had never sinned, took our sin upon Himself and suffered the consequences and paid the price when He died on the cross. And even in the midst of it, He prayed, "Father, forgive them, for they don't know what they are doing" (Luke 23:34 NLT). What a loving Savior! And the best part is He rose to life again—and He offers all who choose Him that same eternal life.

Jesus, I can never, ever thank You enough for what You have done for me! Amen.

Two Criminals

One of the criminals hanging beside [Jesus] scoffed, "So you're the Messiah, are you? Prove it by saving yourself—and us, too, while you're at it!" But the other criminal protested, "Don't you fear God even when you have been sentenced to die? We deserve to die for our crimes, but this man hasn't done anything wrong." Then he said, "Jesus, remember me when you come into your Kingdom." And Jesus replied, "I assure you, today you will be with me in paradise."
LUKE 23:39–43 NLT

Jesus offers anyone His forgiveness of sins up until the very last moment of life, just like we see in the example of the criminals on crosses on either side of Him. The one man was too proud to admit sin and just scoffed at Jesus. But the other realized that Jesus was being punished even though He had done no wrong. That man admitted his own guilt and humbly asked Jesus to remember him in His kingdom. Jesus will remember, save, and bring into paradise absolutely anyone who realizes their need for Jesus as Savior from their sin.

Jesus, thank You for showing that You want to give grace to everyone—even those crying out to You at the very last moment of life here on earth. Amen.

Risen Savior

The angel spoke to the women. "Don't be afraid!" he said. "I know you are looking for Jesus, who was crucified. He isn't here! He is risen from the dead, just as he said would happen. Come, see where his body was lying. And now, go quickly and tell his disciples that he has risen from the dead."
MATTHEW 28:5–7 NLT

What incredible surprise the women mourning over Jesus must have had at the angel's words! And then to see Him risen! We can't fully imagine how awesome it was to be there when Jesus rose to life again after His death on the cross. His resurrection is the foundation of our faith. If He hadn't risen to life again, our faith would be totally useless (1 Corinthians 15:14). But He did, and He proved it to many eyewitnesses (1 Corinthians 15:5–7). And so we continue to share our faith with others, hoping more and more people will choose Jesus as their Savior because there is no one else like Him!

Jesus, I'm so thankful You are worthy of my faith. You defeated death, and You are the one true living Savior! Amen.

Not a Ghost

Jesus himself was suddenly standing there among them. "Peace be with you," he said. But the whole group was startled and frightened, thinking they were seeing a ghost! "Why are you frightened?" he asked. "Why are your hearts filled with doubt? Look at my hands. Look at my feet. You can see that it's really me. Touch me and make sure that I am not a ghost, because ghosts don't have bodies."
LUKE 24:36–39 NLT

Of course the disciples thought they saw a ghost at first. Jesus had been crucified and was buried in the tomb. Jesus even showed them He was fully alive and hungry by asking for something to eat. Then he opened their minds to understand the scriptures by saying, "Yes, it was written long ago that the Messiah would suffer and die and rise from the dead on the third day. It was also written that this message would be proclaimed in the authority of his name to all the nations, beginning in Jerusalem: 'There is forgiveness of sins for all who repent' "(Luke 24:46–47 NLT).

Jesus, I'm so glad I can read about Your disciples' reaction to seeing You alive again! I'm so excited to be with You in heaven someday! Amen.

Let Jesus Refresh You

*"The Lord will guide you continually,
giving you water when you are dry and restoring
your strength. You will be like a well-watered
garden, like an ever-flowing spring."*
ISAIAH 58:11 NLT

What makes you feel worn out and weak and exhausted? Lots of physical activity and very little sleep will do it for sure. And what about on the inside? Sometimes our souls start to feel dry and ugly like near-death plants when we aren't spending good time with Jesus. We need to read His Word, pray, and worship Him so that He can lead and refresh us. He can give us living water so that we never feel dry and thirsty again!

---

*Jesus, thank You for refreshing me
with Your living water! Amen.*

Lies about Jesus

Some of the guards went into the city and told the leading priests what had happened. A meeting with the elders was called, and they decided to give the soldiers a large bribe. They told the soldiers, "You must say, 'Jesus' disciples came during the night while we were sleeping, and they stole his body.' If the governor hears about it, we'll stand up for you so you won't get in trouble." So the guards accepted the bribe and said what they were told to say. Their story spread widely among the Jews, and they still tell it today.
MATTHEW 28:11–15 NLT

Since there were so many eyewitnesses to Jesus' resurrection (read 1 Corinthians 15:5–7), isn't it crazy how so many people didn't believe and still don't believe He actually rose to life again? We believe historical facts about all kinds of other things. But this was an astounding miracle, and our enemy, Satan, doesn't want people to believe in Jesus' resurrection and be saved from sins. This passage in Matthew shows us one way Satan deceived people—with a lie that was spread about Jesus' body being stolen. And sadly, that lie is still spreading today.

Jesus, I pray that people will truly choose to trust in You as their risen Savior. Amen.

Jesus' Great Commission

Jesus came and told his disciples, "I have been given all authority in heaven and on earth. Therefore, go and make disciples of all the nations, baptizing them in the name of the Father and the Son and the Holy Spirit. Teach these new disciples to obey all the commands I have given you. And be sure of this: I am with you always, even to the end of the age."
MATTHEW 28:18–20 NLT

After Jesus rose again, He gave His disciples their assignments—to go out and get their group to grow! It's often called the "great commission." Jesus told His disciples to keep sharing the good news about Him, teaching about His commands, and baptizing people in the name of the Father, Son, and Holy Spirit. As we follow these instructions today, we help more and more people choose Jesus as Savior and live their lives for Him.

Jesus, please help me to obey Your great commission and help others follow You! Amen.

The Whole World Can't Contain

The disciples saw Jesus do many other miraculous signs in addition to the ones recorded in this book. But these are written so that you may continue to believe that Jesus is the Messiah, the Son of God, and that by believing in him you will have life by the power of his name.
JOHN 20:30–31 NLT

After sharing that amazing statement toward the end of his Gospel, John then goes on to say, "Jesus also did many other things. If they were all written down, I suppose the whole world could not contain the books that would be written" (John 21:25 NLT). Wow! Even after all that John has written about Jesus, he says that's just a small sampling and that not even the entire world could contain all the stories! That's so fantastic to think about! We know and love an incredible, powerful Savior—too wonderful for our minds to really comprehend.

Jesus, You are awesome beyond my best imagination. I believe in You and all Your miracles. It is the very best gift to be loved and saved by You! Thank You! Amen.

Hope Despite a Hard Truth

"For God so loved the world that He gave His only begotten Son, that whoever believes in Him should not perish but have everlasting life."
JOHN 3:16 NKJV

A hard truth to accept is that every single one of us will die someday, and none of us knows when that will be. That's why knowing Jesus as Savior is so important. Only He can promise us eternal life because only He rose to life again after dying for our sin. While death is so sad here on earth for those left behind, Jesus gives hope. There is great joy and peace in trusting that every person who believes in Him as the one and only Savior will be in heaven forever in a perfect new body that will never, ever die again.

Jesus, thank You for the hope of heaven for all who trust in You. Please help me share about You with others so more people know You as Savior and will have eternal life. Amen.

Jesus Is the Beginning and End

*"I am the First and the Last.
I am the beginning and the end."*
REVELATION 22:13 NLV

Jesus says several times in the Bible that He is the first and the last, the beginning and the end. (Look at these scriptures too: Isaiah 44:6, Isaiah 48:12, Hebrews 12:2, Revelation 1:8, and Revelation 21:6.) Some Bible translations use the words *Alpha* and *Omega*, which are the names of the first and last letters in the Greek alphabet. To say that He is both of these letters is a way of saying that Jesus is everything and that He has always existed. He has gone before us, and He knows what is behind us. He is always around us. It's hard for our minds to comprehend this reality, but it's wonderful to trust that Jesus knows and has always known the whole story of every one of our lives.

---

*Jesus, You are the beginning and end of all
things. There is no one else like You! I'm so glad
I've chosen to trust You as my Savior. Amen.*

The Way You Give Is the Way You Receive

[Jesus said:] "Give, and it will be given to you. You will have more than enough. It can be pushed down and shaken together and it will still run over as it is given to you. The way you give to others is the way you will receive in return."
LUKE 6:38 NLV

Who are the most generous people you can think of? Who are the most selfish? Who would you rather be like? Most of all, do you want to obey what Jesus taught about giving? These are good questions for all of us to ask ourselves regularly. Jesus clearly taught that we should be generous givers! If we're selfish and keep all our blessings for ourselves, we won't see how much God loves to bless those who love and obey Him.

Jesus, please help me to love giving and sharing with others like You taught. Amen.

Make Every Thought Obey Jesus

Take hold of every thought and make it obey Christ.
2 CORINTHIANS 10:5 NLV

We live in a world with many people who don't love Jesus. Sometimes we spend too much time studying what they do and say and think—especially through television, movies, the Internet, and social media—and soon that seems to be all that's filling our minds. We even start to copy them and go along with trends that go against God's ways and His Word. If that's happening, we need a renewal of our minds, and we can ask Jesus for help as we seek to take hold of every one of our thoughts and make them obey Him. The Bible says, "Do not act like the sinful people of the world. Let God change your life. First of all, let Him give you a new mind. Then you will know what God wants you to do. And the things you do will be good and pleasing and perfect" (Romans 12:2 NLV).

Jesus, please renew my mind. Please help me take every thought and refocus it on You and the good things You want for my life! Amen.

Choose to Trust His Timing

*Dear friends, remember this one thing,
with the Lord one day is as 1,000 years, and 1,000
years are as one day. The Lord is not slow about
keeping His promise as some people think.
He is waiting for you. The Lord does not want any
person to be punished forever. He wants all people
to be sorry for their sins and turn from them.*
2 PETER 3:8–9 NLV

Our Lord is so much bigger and better than what our brains can understand—including the way He views time. This scripture shows us why we need to be patient when it seems like He isn't keeping His promises. He is not being slow or ignoring us. His main goal is to save as many people as possible from their sins and give them eternal life in paradise, and He is doing everything with perfect plans. We can choose to trust His timing and pray that more and more people choose Him too.

---

*Jesus, I'm sorry I have trouble waiting on You
sometimes. Please keep reminding me how
much You love all people and how perfect
Your plans and timing always are. Amen.*

Pray Persistently

Jesus told his disciples a story about how they should keep on praying and never give up: In a town there was once a judge who didn't fear God or care about people. In that same town there was a widow who kept going to the judge and saying, "Make sure that I get fair treatment in court." For a while the judge refused to do anything. Finally, he said to himself, "Even though I don't fear God or care about people, I will help this widow because she keeps on bothering me. If I don't help her, she will wear me out." The Lord said: Think about what that crooked judge said. Won't God protect his chosen ones who pray to him day and night? Won't he be concerned for them? He will surely hurry and help them.
Luke 18:1–8 CEV

Jesus gave us this example to teach us to pray with persistence—don't stop! The point is that if a judge in the courts who did not even respect God was finally willing to help the woman who kept asking and asking, how much more will God help His people who keep asking for His help?

Jesus, I'm so very thankful that You never get tired of my prayers. Amen.

Remember the Reasons

I passed on to you what was most important and what had also been passed on to me. Christ died for our sins, just as the Scriptures said. He was buried, and he was raised from the dead on the third day, just as the Scriptures said. He was seen by Peter and then by the Twelve. After that, he was seen by more than 500 of his followers at one time, most of whom are still alive, though some have died. Then he was seen by James and later by all the apostles. Last of all, as though I had been born at the wrong time, I also saw him.
1 CORINTHIANS 15:3–8 NLT

Like the apostle Paul did, it's so good to write and remember the main reasons for our faith and hope in Jesus Christ. The gospel message and the proof with eyewitnesses of our risen Savior are the best news we can ever know and share!

Jesus, You are alive, and I praise You! I don't ever want to get over how awesome the message of the gospel is. What You did to save all people who choose to repent from sin and believe in You is astounding! Help me to never forget it and never stop sharing it with others. Amen.

Citizen of Heaven

Our citizenship is in heaven. And we eagerly await a Savior from there, the Lord Jesus Christ, who, by the power that enables him to bring everything under his control, will transform our lowly bodies so that they will be like his glorious body.
PHILIPPIANS 3:20–21 NIV

The world is constantly changing and so full of drama, and the news can be so scary. So it's *so good* to remember that no matter where we live during our time on earth, our best and ultimate citizenship is in heaven when we have chosen Jesus as our Savior. Our home will be there forever, and there will be no bad drama or reason to fear. It will be perfect paradise in the presence of Jesus.

Jesus, remind me that everything about this world is just temporary. But forever, I'm a citizen of Your perfect heaven. I'm eagerly watching the sky, so excited for the day when You return. Amen.

Good Reminders

The Holy Spirit will come and help you, because the Father will send the Spirit to take my place. The Spirit will teach you everything and will remind you of what I said while I was with you. I give you peace, the kind of peace only I can give. It isn't like the peace this world can give. So don't be worried or afraid.
JOHN 14:26–27 CEV

Jesus understands that we are forgetful sometimes. He taught that the Holy Spirit would come to both teach us and remind us of all the things He said. He knows we need constant encouragement and reminders of truth. Think how hard it would be to keep on track with God's Word in our culture today if we didn't have the Spirit constantly encouraging us to remember it!

Jesus, I'm so grateful for the Holy Spirit teaching me and reminding me of all that You said. It's so good to have You with me all the time. Amen.

Even When You Can't See

[Jesus] said to Thomas, "Put your finger here; see my hands. Reach out your hand and put it into my side. Stop doubting and believe." Thomas said to him, "My Lord and my God!" Then Jesus told him, "Because you have seen me, you have believed; blessed are those who have not seen and yet have believed."
JOHN 20:27–29 NIV

Can you relate to the disciple Thomas? We all can sometimes. He just wanted to see in person, with his own eyes, that Jesus was alive. And Jesus blessed Thomas by coming to him. Yet Jesus also said, "Blessed are those who have not seen and yet have believed." That includes you and me, and it encourages us to keep the faith.

Jesus, I admit that it's hard sometimes to keep my faith since I didn't get to be there in Bible times and see You with my own eyes. But even when I can't see with my eyes, I choose to believe You are alive and You love me. You have shown me Your presence and Your work in my life through the Holy Spirit. You are the one and only Savior, and I love You! Amen.

Jesus Heals Both Now and Forever

Many demon-possessed people were brought to Jesus. He cast out the evil spirits with a simple command, and he healed all the sick.
MATTHEW 8:16 NLT

Jesus proved that He truly was God with His amazing power to heal and cast out demons. He still has the power to heal today, and we can pray for healing for people who need it. But we can't forget that sometimes God chooses not to heal here on earth. Healing in heaven is far better because it will last forever. So, even more important than praying for healing on earth is to pray that the people who need healing choose Jesus as Savior so they can be healed in heaven forever with eternal life. As we do pray for healing, we can do it with great faith, knowing that God is absolutely able; but we must ask for it according to His will, knowing He *always* does what is right and good, and He can see the bigger picture.

Jesus, You have the power to heal and perform any miracle! Please give me wisdom as I pray for Your will to be done. Amen.

175

Energize and Reenergize

God saved you by his grace when you believed. And you can't take credit for this; it is a gift from God. Salvation is not a reward for the good things we have done, so none of us can boast about it. For we are God's masterpiece. He has created us anew in Christ Jesus, so we can do the good things he planned for us long ago.
EPHESIANS 2:8–10 NLT

If you're ever feeling blah and unmotivated about life, let Ephesians 2:8–10 energize you—and keep coming back to it anytime you need to be reenergized. When you think about how you have the gift of salvation because you chose Jesus Christ and because God created you on purpose with good plans for your life, you should feel full of gratitude and enthusiasm! You should be eager to keep choosing Jesus and following Him. You should be asking Him to guide you in doing all those good things He has ready and scheduled for you in His perfect timing.

Jesus, as I follow You, I'm so excited for You to show me all the good things You want me to do with my life. Day by day, I'll trust You as You guide me. Amen.

Choose Jesus "Even If"

*Even if an army gathers against me,
my heart will not be afraid. Even if war
rises against me, I will be sure of You.*
PSALM 27:3 NLV

Let this scripture inspire you to think of all kinds of "even if" statements to affirm how you will keep on choosing Jesus as your source of courage and strength and love and salvation.

- 🌺 "Even if this test tomorrow is so hard, I will trust You to help me do my best, Jesus!"

- 🌺 "Even if this sickness does not go away, I know You love and care for me in the middle of it, Jesus!"

- 🌺 "Even if you don't heal this injury here on earth like I know You can, I trust that You heal forever in heaven, Jesus!"

- 🌺 "Even if I make mistakes, I know You love and forgive me, Jesus!"

---

*Jesus, thank You that I don't need to be
anxious or afraid of anything and that I
can be totally sure of You! Amen.*

Forgive and Be Forgiven

"When you stand to pray, if you have anything against anyone, forgive him. Then your Father in heaven will forgive your sins also. If you do not forgive them their sins, your Father in heaven will not forgive your sins."
MARK 11:25–26 NLV

Jesus taught that when we want God to listen to and answer our prayers, we need His forgiveness of our sins. And we also need to forgive others for how they've hurt or offended us. This is so important. God loves giving grace and forgiveness, and He wants us to do it too. We are to imitate Him as best we can! To give forgiveness proves how much we understand and appreciate the fact that we have been forgiven of sin. We should be so very grateful and so very generous.

---

*Jesus, I want to forgive freely and generously.
You are so full of mercy and kindness,
and I want to imitate You! Amen.*

Look to Jesus

Let us keep running in the race that God has planned for us. Let us keep looking to Jesus. Our faith comes from Him and He is the One Who makes it perfect. He did not give up when He had to suffer shame and die on a cross. He knew of the joy that would be His later. Now He is sitting at the right side of God.
HEBREWS 12:1–2 NLV

Jesus was able to endure suffering on the cross because of the joy that He was looking forward to later. And if we've chosen Jesus as Savior, we also have incredible joy waiting for us in heaven. There's joy along the way here on earth, too, even in the midst of suffering and sorrow we might experience. Can you make a list or journal about it? It's a great idea to keep track of all the joys and blessings, big and small, that God gives us to help encourage us along the life He has mapped out for us.

Jesus, I'll keep looking to You. Thank You for the joys I have now and the forever joy that's ahead! Amen.

You Will Be Weird in This World

Dear friends, your real home is not here on earth. You are strangers here. I ask you to keep away from all the sinful desires of the flesh. These things fight to get hold of your soul.
1 PETER 2:11 NLV

It's weird to be a true Christian in this world—and that's a good thing, because God's Word tells us to expect it. So just embrace the weirdness. Some versions of 1 Peter 2:11 describe Christians as being like aliens on earth in the sense that we are strangers here because this world is not our real home. When we choose Jesus as Savior, we know that He will give us eternal life someday in heaven, which *is* our real home. So we should be careful not to follow what the world says is right if it goes against what God says is right. Being a true Christian isn't always easy, but it is always totally worth it!

Jesus, no matter how weird I feel, help me to follow Your ways and wisdom more than anything in this world, because I know my real home is in heaven with You. Amen.

Choose Jesus Morning, Noon, and Night

I ask for your help, Lord God, and you will keep me safe. Morning, noon, and night you hear my concerns and my complaints. I am attacked from all sides, but you will rescue me unharmed by the battle. You have always ruled, and you will hear me.

PSALM 55:16–19 CEV

This psalm reminds us that there is never a bad time to cry out to Jesus. We can choose to pray anytime: morning, noon, and evening—and every moment in between, plus all night long. He wants to be included in our lives 24-7. He wants us to tell Him our needs and depend on Him to help. He never gets tired of our prayers. We have such an awesome and loving Lord and Savior.

Jesus, thank You for being available every single moment of every single day to listen to me! Amen.

Deep Roots

As you have put your trust in Christ Jesus the Lord to save you from the punishment of sin, now let Him lead you in every step. Have your roots planted deep in Christ. Grow in Him. Get your strength from Him. Let Him make you strong in the faith as you have been taught. Your life should be full of thanks to Him.
COLOSSIANS 2:6–7 NLV

The deeper a plant's roots go, the stronger it is. And the deeper you grow roots in Jesus, the stronger you are too! Learn from Jesus and follow His ways, and thank God every day for His many blessings.

Jesus, please lead me in every step of my life. Please help my roots grow so deeply in You that my faith becomes incredibly strong. Thank You for so many wonderful blessings in my life. Amen.

Dreams of Heaven

Then I saw a new heaven and a new earth.... I heard a loud shout from the throne, saying, "Look, God's home is now among his people! He will live with them, and they will be his people.... He will wipe every tear from their eyes, and there will be no more death or sorrow or crying or pain...." And the one sitting on the throne said, "Look, I am making everything new!"
REVELATION 21:1, 3–5 NLT

When we've chosen Jesus as Savior and know that we'll spend forever in heaven someday, it's fun to dream about what heaven might be like and what our loved ones who are already there are doing. But we also always need to remember that nobody here on earth knows a whole lot about it yet. The Bible doesn't give much detail about heaven, probably because our minds couldn't fully understand how awesome it will be (1 Corinthians 2:9). But it does tell us that everything will be new and that there will be no more death or sorrow or crying or pain. Those facts alone show us how awesome it will be!

Jesus, I'm so grateful for You and for the hope of heaven. Amen.

Share the Good News

I am not ashamed of this Good News about Christ. It is the power of God at work, saving everyone who believes—the Jew first and also the Gentile. This Good News tells us how God makes us right in his sight.
ROMANS 1:16–17 NLT

We should all want to be able to say this scripture honestly—that we are not embarrassed or ashamed of the good news that Jesus came to earth to live a perfect life and teach us, died on the cross to pay for our sins, rose to life again, and offers us eternal life too. When we share this with others, we help spread God's power to save people from their sins.

Jesus, please help me to never be embarrassed or ashamed to share the good news about You and how You want to save everyone who chooses You! Thank You for loving all people and wanting to rescue us all from sin! Amen.

Look Up and Ahead

Since you have been raised to new life with Christ, set your sights on the realities of heaven, where Christ sits in the place of honor at God's right hand. Think about the things of heaven, not the things of earth. For you died to this life, and your real life is hidden with Christ in God. And when Christ, who is your life, is revealed to the whole world, you will share in all his glory.
COLOSSIANS 3:1–4 NLT

When Jesus took the punishment for our sin on the cross, He did not stay dead but rose again. And when you believe in Him as your Savior, you have been raised spiritually from the death that sin causes and have the gift of forever life in heaven with Jesus. No matter what hard things are going on in your life, keep looking up and ahead for the awesome things of heaven that are coming your way!

Jesus, help me to keep my eyes and mind up and ahead, always thinking about You and Your love and all the good blessings that come from You in heaven. Amen.

When He Returns

The Spirit teaches you everything you need to know, and what he teaches is true—it is not a lie. So just as he has taught you, remain in fellowship with Christ. And now, dear children, remain in fellowship with Christ so that when he returns, you will be full of courage and not shrink back from him in shame.
1 JOHN 2:27–28 NLT

As Christians, we're supposed to be ready for Jesus to return to earth at any moment. (Look up Matthew 24:44 and Luke 12:40.) To some people, that might sound silly or scary, but for those of us who love Jesus and stay close to Him, it should be exciting! It should fill us with hope and joy! God's Word promises that if we remain in fellowship with Jesus, we will be full of courage and not shrink back with fear or be ashamed in any way when Jesus returns to earth.

Jesus, I believe You will return right on Your perfect schedule. I'm watching and waiting! I want to stay so close to You. Amen.

Thank You, Jesus

As he was going into a village, ten men who had leprosy met him. They stood at a distance and called out in a loud voice, "Jesus, Master, have pity on us!" When he saw them, he said, "Go, show yourselves to the priests." And as they went, they were cleansed. One of them, when he saw he was healed, came back, praising God in a loud voice. He threw himself at Jesus' feet and thanked him—and he was a Samaritan. Jesus asked, "Were not all ten cleansed? Where are the other nine?"
LUKE 17:12–17 NIV

This account in Luke 17 reminds us how important it is to say thank you, especially to Jesus. These ten men had been miraculously healed by Jesus. You'd think they would have been bursting with gratitude, yet only one of them turned back to Jesus to actually thank and worship Him. In whatever ways God blesses us, we should always want to be like the one man and not the other nine!

Jesus, please forgive me when I forget to thank You! I am so grateful for You giving me salvation and life, and I want to worship and praise You for everything. Amen.

Others Should Notice

[Jesus said:] "You must love each other, just as I have loved you. If you love each other, everyone will know that you are my disciples."
JOHN 13:34–35 CEV

If we've chosen Jesus as Savior and we're regularly spending time in God's Word and learning at church, we should be doing what Jesus taught in the Bible, and others should notice. We should be known for loving God first and loving others as ourselves. We should be known for being generous and helping take care of the needy. We should be known as praying people. We should be known as people who share God's truth and encourage others. We should be known as honest, fair, and kind. We should never pretend to be perfect people, but we should point others to Jesus as the only one who is perfect.

Jesus, I want others to notice that I love You and I follow You so that they will want to love and follow You too. Please help me show them in the best kind of ways. Amen.

Be Patient and Persevere

Be willing to wait for the Lord to come again. Learn from the farmer. He waits for the good fruit from the earth until the early and late rains come. You must be willing to wait also.... See how the early preachers spoke for the Lord by their suffering and by being willing to wait. We think of those who stayed true to Him as happy even though they suffered. You have heard how long Job waited. You have seen what the Lord did for him in the end. The Lord is full of loving-kindness and pity.
JAMES 5:7–8, 10–11 NLV

Sometimes we grow tired, impatient, and discouraged while following Jesus in a world that seems darker each day. But as this scripture reminds us, the Lord is full of compassion and mercy. He cares, and He sees our faithfulness. We can look back to examples of those who persevered before us and were greatly blessed and be encouraged to keep going strong as we follow Jesus and wait for His return.

Jesus, with Your help, I will continue to be patient and persevere until You return one day. Amen.

Put It into Practice

Jesus replied, "But even more blessed are all who hear the word of God and put it into practice."
LUKE 11:28 NLT

It's easy to hear or read something but not really "get it." And it's easy to not actually *do* anything with what we learn. Jesus knew this was true of everyone, and He said we were blessed when we both heard God's Word *and* put it into practice. The Bible also teaches this in James 1:22–25 (NLT): "Don't just listen to God's word. You must do what it says. Otherwise, you are only fooling yourselves. For if you listen to the word and don't obey, it is like glancing at your face in a mirror. You see yourself, walk away, and forget what you look like. But if you look carefully into the perfect law that sets you free, and if you do what it says and don't forget what you heard, then God will bless you for doing it."

Jesus, please help me to not just hear and learn from You and Your Word; help me do what I'm learning. I want to live my life for You. Amen.

God's Holy One

Because of what Jesus said, many of his disciples turned their backs on him and stopped following him. Jesus then asked his twelve disciples if they also were going to leave him. Simon Peter answered, "Lord, there is no one else that we can go to! Your words give eternal life. We have faith in you, and we are sure that you are God's Holy One."
JOHN 6:66–69 CEV

Jesus' teaching and the Bible can feel overwhelming at times. Even some disciples who spent all their time learning from Jesus decided to turn their backs on Jesus and stop following Him because of things He said. But Simon Peter was committed to Jesus and loyal. And even if he didn't always fully understand, He was certain that Jesus was the Holy One of God and that His words gave eternal life. And we can be certain of that too. So when we're feeling confused, we can let this scripture in John 6 encourage us. We can pray like this:

Jesus, I have faith in You as my one and only Savior, no matter what, and I'm positive You are the Holy One of God! I will choose to keep learning from You all of my days. Amen.

About the Author

JoAnne Simmons is a writer and editor who's in awe of God's love and the ways He guides and provides. Her favorite things include coffee shops, libraries, the Bible, good grammar, being a wife and mom, dogs, music, road trips, punctuation, church, the beach, and many dear family and friends—but not in that order. If her family weren't so loving and flexible, she'd be in big trouble; and if God's mercies weren't new every morning, she'd never get out of bed.